with warm greetings

from South Africa

Anneke and Ingrid

2012

MAN
OF
THE
PEOPLE

MAN OF THE PEOPLE

A photographic tribute to Nelson Mandela

PETER MAGUBANE

PAN MACMILLAN
AND
MUTLOATSE ARTS HERITAGE TRUST

This publication was made possible with the generous support of ArcelorMittal

AUTHOR ACKNOWLEDGEMENT

Peter Magubane would like to acknowledge the hard work done by Luanne Michell and David Meyer-Gollan.

First published in 2008 by

Pan Macmillan South Africa
Private Bag x19, Northlands 2116
www.panmacmillan.co.za

and

Mutloatse Arts Heritage Trust
101B Killarney Mall Office Tower
Riviera Road, Houghton
PO Box 2599, Houghton 2041
mutloatse@mweb.co.za
www.mutloatse.com

The publishers would like to thank their media sponsors, Alive Advertising.

ISBN 978 1 77010 065 7

ACKNOWLEDGEMENTS

The publishers would like to thank Zindzi Mandela for permission to reproduce her poem.
Some of the photographs in this book previously appeared in *Mandela, Man of Destiny*, published by Don Nelson (1996).
Every effort has been made to contact copyright holders. Those copyright holders whom we have been unable to contact should contact the publishers so that the omission may be remedied.

Design and layout: Kevin Shenton, Triple M Design
Design concept: Peter Bosman
Image retouching: Amichai Tahor and Andreas Vlachakis, Lightfarm
Editor: Andrea Nattrass
Printed and bound in South Africa by Ultra Litho

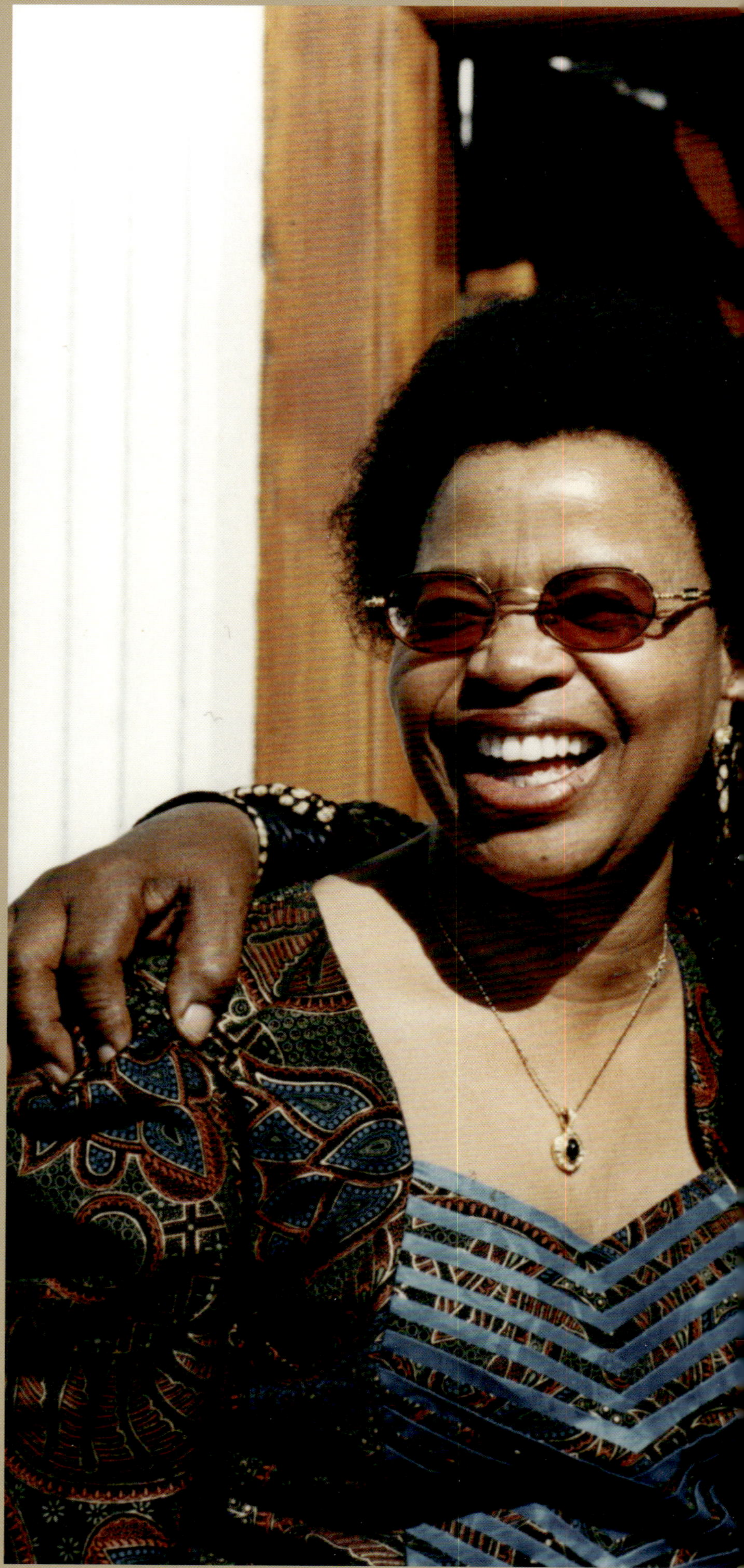

CONTENTS

Speaking at the launch of the National Campaign for Learning and Teaching

Nelson Mandela said, 'We are obliged to make it possible for everyone

to develop their potential to the full; to provide opportunities for everyone

to learn and nurture their talent.' Our global commitment extends beyond the bottom line,

to the people and the communities in whom we invest.

ArcelorMittal shares Mandela's vision to develop young minds. In South Africa alone,

we have committed ninety per cent of our Corporate Social Investment spend to education.

LAKSHMI MITTAL
ARCELORMITTAL CHAIRMAN AND CEO

I dedicate this book to my late parents.

TO MY FATHER

who gave me my first camera,

a Kodak Box Brownie, which I used to take pictures at school.

TO MY MOTHER

who made sure I did not linger around the street corners of Sophiatown.

She wanted me to achieve what I am today.

PETER MAGUBANE

Peter Magubane (photographed by Bob Gosa-ni) is accosted by police outside the Drill Hall, Johannesburg, during the first days of the Treason Trial in 1956.

THROUGH THE LENS OF A RESILIENT STORYTELLER

Melanie Lawrence

In the words of Nelson Mandela, Peter Magubane's photo stories on apartheid, 'helped pave the way to transformation in South Africa'. Along the way, Peter has endured great personal sacrifices and yet this formidable man continues in his 54th year of photography to document the 'day to day life of people'.

Sophiatown, 2008. As Peter drives through Sophiatown en route to Soweto, he recalls his childhood spent on her streets. The old mining-town-style houses, built on the ruins of Sophiatown for the white suburb of Triomf ('Triumph'), stand on soil that is historically loaded. It's hard to imagine the legendary days of the Sophiatown that gave birth to activists and artists such as Peter. Those streets own his boyhood memories: the first camera his father gave to him, his mother's love and discipline, the matchbox home his family filled, being stabbed one day while out playing.

Sophiatown, 1955. It's a Saturday night. The swanky gents and classy dames are out on the town, dressed to the nines. High heels rat-a-tat-tat on the dusty streets. The seductive jazz draws you into a nearby shebeen. Inside foot-tapping saxophones and social debates fill the air. In the corner a handsome, 23-year-old Peter discusses news-beats with his *Drum* friends, Can Themba 'the English master' and Bob Gosani 'the brilliant photographer'. In less than a year Peter has worked his way up the magazine's ranks from driver to photojournalist. These three are some of the many stars that Sof'town has raised. While others have chosen the political platform to confront the social injustices of apartheid, Peter has chosen the camera.

He reveals, 'I wanted to document the lives of black South Africans at the time. That was what drove me to photography.' The Peter back in 1955 has no idea what the years ahead have in store for him.

He arrives in Soweto today through zigzagging back roads. Peter is scouting the scrap heaps and coal yards for underage child workers. He's finishing the final shots for his book covering decades of child labour in South Africa, from as early as the 1950s to the present. This is just one of his many current projects. His sturdy frame is strong and seems much younger than his 76 years. His presence owns the space it occupies. The same passion that led him to expose the atrocities of the apartheid years continues to drive him to portray the social struggles of today.

Return with Peter to the late 1950s. He is making his mark on the world. Recently he has covered his first big assignment, on the African National Congress (ANC), for *Drum* magazine. The editor Tom Hopkinson is very satisfied with the young cameraman's work. Peter will continue to work on exposés with *Drum* writers, such as the 'Nude "Pass" Parade' covering the degrading pass laws and the treatment of black people in South Africa.

The following year, Peter wins first and third place in a photographic competition. The white photographer who takes second place refuses to shake his hand. Despite the rampant prejudices of the period, an unstoppable career is launched. At the same time, Sophiatown is being desecrated, torn to the ground. Along with the other families, his is forcibly removed – uprooted and relocated to Diepkloof.

He drives into the Sowetan scrap yard. It's a metal graveyard. Giant rusting teeth bite into the air. Magubane is looking for the young boys who work here. They abandon school to earn as little as five rand a day collecting and selling scrap metal. 'Many of them are playing truant, and don't understand the value of education,' he tries to explain the complicated issue.

Magubane often goes beyond the camera to help the people he photographs. Over the years he has helped to reunite many runaways with their parents. He explains he will not interfere until, 'They come to me "Madala! Madala!" they call me, "I want to go home."' Only five of the thirty-five boys and girls he has helped have returned to the streets.

During the 1960s, youth in other parts of the world are expressing liberation through music and protests. On home soil, the photojournalist, now in his thirties, is covering momentous events such as the Sharpeville massacre – 'I had never seen so many dead people' – and the Rivonia Trial for *Drum* magazine.

It is painful to bring up the past, but he does so graciously. 'Often in my work I would find a person struggling, even dying', but the photographs came first. 'It was only after, when I got home, that I would ask myself "what are you doing?".' But the next morning, it was back on the streets with camera in hand. He was driven by the belief that, 'The world will respond!'

He reaches his next stop. It's off the tar road and into the heart of the Jabulani coal yard. Miniature mountains of depressing nuggets block out the surrounding world. Squat make-do homes sit sadly on the grit. A young mother hangs bright clothing on a line, while a baby boy plays in the sooty muck. Chicken cages are piled up everywhere and a few escapees run in clucking circles. A bitter smell saturates the air.

Starting as early as sunrise, youths shovel heavy coal for donkey-cart deliveries across Soweto. In winter the township's skylines are smudged by coal fires. 'It's warmer here and they have shelter.' Magubane looks out the window. Exploited and devastatingly poor, the biggest issue facing these children today he feels is, 'Without a doubt, education. Without education, you can do nothing!'

A tough-looking man recognises the photographer. 'He's one of my boys,' Magubane cheers. 'He has been working here for years.' It's poignant that the boy he photographed in the 1970s is his lead to the coal youths of today. He's made his contact, so he leaves this Armageddon

Under arrest: Peter Magubane arrested for taking photographs in Alexandra Township in 1988.

moonscape for the livelier streets of Zola. Teenagers decorate the curbs and parks. He overtakes a withering woman driving her wheelchair in the left-hand lane.

Sometimes Magubane's work steps on toes. When he does get threats, he says very firmly, 'I don't take threats!' He is a stubborn man, who is angered when he doesn't get his own way. Most people find themselves backing down to his authority. After all, he has gone up against the Nationalist government and prevailed. There's not much that can intimidate Peter Magubane.

An otherwise normal day in June 1969 is life-changing for the newsman. The brutal fist of censorship strikes down hard. It's not the first time he's been harassed by the police, but this time he is dragged off

to Pretoria Central Prison. There he is interrogated by the police. They demand he tell them if he 'has been sent by the communists to put South Africa in a bad light'.

Made to stand for five days and five nights on unstable bricks, Peter collapses on the fifth day. He is kept in solitary confinement until October 1969, when he is charged under the Suppression of Communism Act. The onslaught of charges continues. In February 1970, after being acquitted of the charges, he is re-arrested immediately, in court. They continue to detain him in solitary confinement. In August 1970, he is charged again, under the Terrorism Act, and once more in March 1971, under Section Six of the Terrorism Act – allowing for his indefinite detention. Finally he is released in 1971. Peter spent a total of 586 days in solitary confinement.

He was forced to resign from the *Rand Daily Mail* and while still under a five-year banning order in 1972, he breaks it and serves another six months in prison. 'I have paid a price for being a photographer in this country,' he shares.

As soon as the banning order expired in October 1975, he is back on his news beat with the *Rand Daily Mail*. 'No one was going to stop me from telling the truth!'

With poise he explains how he found ways and means of surviving in solitary confinement. His strength came 'from God', he opens up, 'and I knew that I had done absolutely nothing wrong! All I had done was to photograph the children working on farms.' He recollects, 'I could hear the other prisoners scream right through the night, being tortured.'

'If I had thought I was the only one, I would have gone cuckoo. It helped me a great deal to know I was not the only one suffering. There were others suffering worse than me, on Robben Island, serving life sentences.' Today he is a calm man who is quick to laugh, and it's clear he hasn't allowed resentment to fill his heart. 'Don't forget, but forgive. You have to go on with your life.'

Today the main intersection of Dube is a bustling, multi-layered whirl of twenty-first century township life in South Africa. Magubane joins a patient queue to buy mealies.

He chats about development in Soweto: the new Maponya Mall and the stadium construction, the crumbling curbs and non-existent pavements, the people who are still without houses. He passionately comments, 'You cannot separate people from politics.'

The day is 16 June 1976. In the lead-up to this day, a phenomenon has swept the land. Word has spread like invisible fire. The black youth guard a secret closely. Not even their teachers or parents know about the planned march. The nation will be shocked this cold winter morning, as news leaks of the protest against inferior Bantu education and Afrikaans as the medium of instruction. It starts in Soweto, spreads to Alexandra, next to Pretoria, and so its flames extend.

When journalists are prohibited from entering Soweto, Peter is on the scene, equipment loaded. A soldier with a camera. In the distance he sees sinister black smoke, a signal of action on the ground. He moves between these sites.

Magubane has more photographs of 16 June than any other photographer. Black and white images of the schoolchildren fleeing from the hail of bullets intended to kill them. Mixed emotions of terror and liberation saturate their faces. It is a powerful turning point in a land of oppression, forever recorded by Peter's shutter.

On one occasion, while Peter is covering the continuing uprising, the police assault the cameraman and break his nose. They tell him to expose his film to light, to destroy the images. Peter is more concerned about losing the images than his bloody face. The world needs to see the undeniable horror, the brutal madness of apartheid captured on film.

Later that year, when the police incite the Mzimhlope Hostel dwellers to attack the township residents Peter works into the night covering the violence. As he passes his Diepkloof home on his way to the paper's offices he sees his home ablaze. He is powerless as he watches the building crackle to the earth. Again in August 1976, he is detained for 123 days with other black newsmen – another futile government attempt to prevent his work from exposing the atrocities of apartheid.

As he passes the tourist queues outside Madiba's old shoebox home in Orlando West, spilling into Vilakazi Street, conversation turns to the focus of this book: Peter's relationship with Nelson Mandela and particularly the time, between 1990 and 1994, spent as Mandela's official photographer.

Recently Peter donated over a hundred photographs of those prominent years to Nelson Mandela. 'I wanted to thank Madiba for trusting me, and allowing me the opportunity to document that part of his life.'

Magubane remembers his innocuous first meeting with the man who would later be counted as a lifelong friend. 'It was during the days when Mandela was practising law. I needed an attorney to represent my father who had been involved in a car accident, so I went to Mandela and Tambo's offices,' he recalls. 'At that time I didn't know how involved they were in the politics of the country. Mandela told me that he was too busy and didn't want to take on too many cases, as he was finishing off work that they already had. I had to find another lawyer.'

Over time, Peter's children become friends with the Mandela children because they go to the same school in Swaziland. 'I was able to provide transport for them to school, as I knew that their mother [Winnie Madikizela-Mandela] couldn't do that because she was also banned. Fortunately I had people I could rely on who would not spill the beans,' Peter shares.

Slowly, almost indirectly, a kinship is forged between two politicians – one who speaks with words and actions, the other who speaks with his camera.

Peter subsequently goes to visit Mandela in prison on Robben Island, solidifying the relationship between the then future President and the charismatic cameraman. 'I used a Xhosa pseudonym – Ralanqobuso Mtirara. I don't know how they let me in, but they did. We were both taken aback to see how time had affected our physical appearances but we were both strong warriors at heart,' says Peter. 'Mandela congratulated me on the photographic work that I had been doing in exposing the country without any fear.'

The meeting is brief and conversation difficult as they are watched by two prison officers standing nearby. Still, Peter knows that a vital connection has been made between the two men.

The 1980s open international doors for the photojournalist. An assignment for the United Nations High Commissioner for Refugees expands his cause into Africa. 'Through photography I have seen most parts of the world,' he imparts. The starvation he covers in places like Somalia and Ethiopia in this decade, 'Hits you right on the forehead.'

At the same time, he works for *Time* magazine South Africa. On one assignment, in 1985, he covers a student's funeral in Natalspruit. When violence breaks out on that day he is shot seventeen times below the waist with buckshot. Back out on the beat as soon as possible, in 1986, he steps in to save a mother and daughter from an enraged crowd in Leandra.

On 11 February 1990, Magubane faces bitter disappointment. 'The most historic day in the country's history, when Mandela was released from jail, posed my greatest photographic challenge. A large crowd had gathered outside the Victor Verster prison in Paarl. People had even climbed on top of buses and trucks.'

'Photographers were on the ground and I joined them in trying to find a position to capture those precious moments. Then when Mandela finally walked out, the massive crowd surged forward with such force that we were literally trampled in the frenzy. In my entire career, that was the only crucial photograph that I was unable to capture. I was extremely frustrated and disappointed, but what could I do? The only option was to move on and rest in the knowledge that I was able to shoot other priceless moments.'

The opportunity of a lifetime comes when Peter has another meeting with Mandela. Although he had missed the crucial 'first steps of freedom', Peter is honoured to be selected as Mandela's official photographer to chronicle the country's four-year transition to democracy. 'The kind of "political photography" work that I was doing while they were in jail prepared the way for me to be chosen as the photographer who would follow Mandela around until such time that he became President of South Africa.'

'I was elated!' laughs Peter. 'What more could a photographer want than to be called upon to follow the life of a saint? It was wonderful to be selected from so many photographers to follow this courageous man. I knew that I must do my best to document his life as I see it, up to the time that he became President.'

Madiba and his grandson, Bambatha, in 1990.

Nelson and Winnie together at home after his release from prison on 11 February 1990.

And so the historical journey begins. Peter is privy to the daily miracle that is unfolding in the lives of South Africans during his four-year tenure as the official photographer. He makes the most of the prime positions available to him at the countless photographic opportunities along the road to a new political dispensation.

Magubane describes how his relationship with Mandela strengthened as they journeyed through the 'passage of peace' together. 'We already trusted each other and shared a mutual respect. As a photographer, as someone who is documenting history, you are not going to be able to tell the truth if you are not able to forgive. During these special years, I learned that one needs to have patience; you need to learn to acknowledge that mistakes are made.'

According to Peter, the main aim of this book is to showcase Mandela's historic journey to the presidency and to show the world the kind of man Mandela is. 'In this book, you will find pictures of Mandela being serious and then he is holding a baby; at other times he is jiving and dancing. This is the man who most white South Africans thought might be different. Instead of confirming their worst fears of pushing them out of the country, he offered hands of peace, saying: "Come, let's work together, let's build this country together."'

There is a sparkle in Peter's eye as he remembers the occasion that led to his favourite photograph in the book, 'It is definitely the one of Mandela dancing at his 72nd birthday celebration taken at Kippies in Newtown, Johannesburg. You can see the joy of freedom shining in his eyes.'

Amidst the many international accolades Peter has received, there is one award that has pride of place on his shelf: the Order for Meritorious Service Class II, which he received from former President Nelson Mandela in 1999. 'I have received many photographic prizes, from this country in the 1950s to numerous international and lifetime achievement awards, but the one I received from Madiba is my most prized possession. When you have an award from a man of Mandela's stature – what more could you want?' he beams.

Peter has published sixteen books, three of which were banned in South Africa in the 1970s and 80s: *Magubane's South Africa*, *Black as I Am* and *Black Child*. During a ceremony in honour of his work the comment was made that 'Many airlines cover less territory than Magubane's solo exhibitions!' His subject-matter is equally wide-ranging, from vanishing cultures to post-democracy life in South Africa.

Our journey ends back at Magubane's home in Johannesburg. His lounge is filled with bright-beaded pots and wooden carvings. In the corner an antique gramophone sits proudly near a black and white photograph of Peter masquerading a trumpet. From behind a straw hat, a beaming young Sophiatown gent strikes a pose.

As he sits in front of a window, light illuminates Peter Magubane's trademark white hair. The image we are left with is of a man whose life's work is inseparable from the weave of more than half a century of South Africa's history.

Melanie Lawrence is an independent writer based in Johannesburg. She specialises in biographical, social and cultural subjects.

Note

Additional interview material was provided by Cheryl Ramurath.

'THE GOODEST MAN IN THE WORLD'

Raymond Louw

Almost as one 1 300 people rose from their seats in the Linder Auditorium at the University of the Witwatersrand's education complex in Johannesburg as a grey-haired man dressed in dark clothes limped on to the stage with his wife holding one arm and an aide the other. The applause was spontaneous and loud.

The man was Nelson Mandela and he was about to introduce the speaker at the fifth Nelson Mandela Lecture, the man who 'had run the world' as Secretary-General of the United Nations (UN) for a decade, Kofi Annan.

The largely South African audience reflected the 'rainbow nation' that Mandela ushered into the country on 10 May 1994 at his inauguration as the first black President of a democratic South Africa. The audience turned its attention later to Annan but for the moment it was Mandela they focused on and lauded.

Mandela, a frail celebrant of his 89th birthday and his 9th wedding anniversary only a few days earlier, acknowledged the applause with what had become his trademark, a generous smile and a wave of the hand.

Throughout the proceedings on Sunday 22 July 2007, the spontaneous acclamation with flashes of adulation lighting the gathering was to occur another three times as Mandela manoeuvred himself to the speaker's platform and then back to his chair and later, after Annan had delivered his measured view of Africa, when he left the stage.

Artists in the theatre never get four standing ovations in one night – one, maybe two at most – but here were four for an ageing man with a beaming smile. Overkill? Hardly, in a country where this man contributed with consummate skill, great courage coupled with sensitivity and understanding to help achieve a relatively peaceful transfer of power from a tyrannical government to an oppressed majority. The process has been called a miracle.

South Africa had been on the brink of civil war with the combustible material merely awaiting someone to strike a match to set off a calamitous, destructive conflagration – a spark ready to hand in the grasp of firebrands lurking in the country, fortunately not in large numbers.

Then Mandela brought his calming voice and influence to bear. After a 27-year history of unjust imprisonment and the brutal oppression of his fellow Africans by the government, he could have exercised the power newly bestowed on him to exact revenge on the former rulers. Instead he chose reconciliation and peaceful coexistence and persuaded others that this course was the only acceptable way forward. It is true that the transfer of power was achieved with the co-operation of the white leader F.W. de Klerk, but without Nelson Mandela and his spirit of inclusiveness, his striving for peace and his leadership qualities, it would not have happened.

Apart from respect for his age and the spirit of reconciliation exuding from him, the audience was also celebrating his dedication to peace and his concern for minorities.

Kofi Annan took full advantage of the occasion honouring Nelson Mandela's name and his humanity by expressing his and his wife Nane's delight at spending 'your birthday here with you in Johannesburg' (on 18 July) and then humorously adding his personal approbation:

It is truly a privilege for me to deliver this year's Mandela Lecture. Before I begin, I want to clarify something. I am delivering a lecture in honour of Nelson Mandela. I am in no way delivering a lecture to Nelson Mandela.

I wouldn't dare.

If I did, I imagine he would listen graciously, tolerantly. But let me tell you this: one does not presume to lecture Madiba. Not on his birthday, not on any other day. He may have relinquished his office years ago, but he has not relinquished one ounce of his natural, personal authority.

Still, for some reason he persists in calling me 'boss'.

For years, whenever I'd call, he would say, 'My boss. How are you, boss?' I'd reply, 'How can I be your boss?' He'd say, 'Secretary-General of the UN. You run the world'. Of course, as he knows, I never did run the world. Now I don't even run the UN. And still he persists. I think he is teasing me.

But then, he has always been like that. You see it in his expansive smile. Nelson Mandela may be the most gentle, good-humoured, even mischievous icon that the world has known. He is also one of the strongest. We all know about his courage and tenacity which saw him through 27 years in prison and saw South Africa through the end of apartheid and a difficult, but successful, transition to freedom.

An ANC rally in Port Elizabeth before the 1994 elections.

The world has seen how deeply he believes in freedom, human dignity, and the right of the individual to fulfil his or her dream. And in our work together, I have been privileged to see how determined he can be in pursuit of those ideals. I have seen him in tough negotiations like those in Burundi, where he was trying to get the warring factions to put down their guns and make peace. When he saw what was going on around him, he said, 'You men make me ashamed to be African.'

A withering indictment from someone who makes us all proud to be African. You can imagine the force of these words. Or perhaps you cannot. It was an extraordinarily powerful moment. And it certainly had its intended effect. On certain points – certain principles – Nelson Mandela cannot be moved.

When his term as President ended, as you know, a lot of people tried to talk him into staying on. But he was determined to leave office. What a wonderful example on a continent where presidents have, in some cases, defied or changed their countries' constitutions and clung to power for decades.

There are other former leaders who have drawn important lessons from Mandela's post-presidency: that the centre stage is not the only place from which you can make a contribution.

Annan went on to describe the unique group assembled by Nelson Mandela in Johannesburg to form an elder statesmens' think tank to try to find solutions to some of the world's intractable problems. Among them were such eminent persons as former United States President Jimmy Carter, former Irish President Mary Robinson, philanthropist and economist Muhammad Yunus, former Chinese Foreign Minister Li Zhaozing, and Annan himself as well as Nelson Mandela's wife, Graça Machel, a leader in education and the welfare of children. Annan put it thus, 'As "elders", so to speak, we have a unique perspective to share, and, we believe, an obligation to share it.'

The project is a world first, a fascinatingly novel exercise in bringing the wisdom, sagacity, experience, statesmanship and political acumen of men and women whose collective lifespan totals more than 1 000 years to bear on the some of the world's most difficult problems.

The initiative was launched by Nelson Mandela together with Archbishop Desmond Tutu and Graça Machel. In doing so on his birthday, Mandela said:

Let us call them Global Elders, not because of their age, but because of their individual and collective wisdom.

This group derives its strength not from political, economic or military power, but from the independence and integrity of those who are here. They do not have careers to build, elections to win, constituencies to please. They can talk to anyone they please and are free to follow paths they deem right, even if hugely unpopular.

He then described how Richard Branson, the man who built the Virgin Atlantic empire and who shares a birthday with Nelson Mandela, and British musician and activist Peter Gabriel put to him their idea of establishing a small, dedicated group of leaders, working objectively and without any vested personal interest in the outcome to solve difficult conflicts facing the world.

'Since then I have watched the concept grow, gain structure and strength and become a real, viable, and pragmatic initiative,' said Mandela. He went further to spell out how he saw them tackling their role:

They will not take the easy, short-term route, but support long-term, sustainable approaches that address the root causes of the problems they tackle.

They are, I know, committed to working with local and indigenous knowledge; to listening and bringing together antagonists and protagonists; to working with anyone who is motivated to resolve a problem. They can help foster and introduce innovative ideas and little known solutions to connect those who have real practical needs with those who have something to give.

Through their friends in business, they can mobilise up to date technology, and raise not only awareness of forgotten issues, but also help locate the resources to address them. But whatever techniques they use, I believe that in the end it is kindness and generous accommodation that are the catalysts for real change. I know these esteemed friends of mine are capable of doing all these things.

Referring to Desmond Tutu, his co-author, as it were, of the enterprise, Mandela went on to say:

And I expect that, if my friend the Archbishop has anything to do with it, they will insist on assuming the essential interdependence of all humankind. We call this the spirit of Ubuntu *– that profound African sense that we are human only through the humanity of other human beings.*

I am confident that the Elders can become a real role model – leading, guiding and supporting all sorts of initiatives, both their own and those of many others. The Elders can speak freely and boldly, working both publicly and behind the scenes on whatever actions need to be taken.

Mandela, though a member of the Elders, gracefully withdrew from active participation. He commented, 'As I have said before, I am trying to take my retirement seriously and I will unfortunately not be able to participate in the really exciting part of their work, analysing problems, seeking solutions, searching out partners.'

Always the hard-headed, practical man with an eye on the sustainability and financial viability of his projects, Mandela announced where the backing for this unique enterprise will come from. He said the Elders would be independently funded by a group of founders, including Richard Branson and Peter Gabriel. And he spoke of the other founders: philanthropists Ray Chambers and Michael Chambers; Bridgeway

Nelson Mandela and Archbishop Desmond Tutu at the Anglican Church in White City, Soweto, shortly after Mandela's release.

It was Peter Gabriel who explained the title:

In traditional societies, the elders always had a role in conflict resolution, long-term thinking and applying wisdom wherever it was needed. We are moving to this global village and yet we don't have our global elders. The Elders can be a group who have [sic] the trust of the world, who can speak freely, be fiercely independent and respond fast and flexibly in conflict situations.

Foundation; Pam Omidyar of Humanity United; Amy Robbins; Shashi Ruia of the billionaire Indian Essar Group; Dick Tarlow; and The United Nations Foundation.

The Group will meet at least twice a year. Mary Robinson pointed out that its work had already started with one of the first issues to be tackled being human rights. The Elders noted that the Universal Declaration of Human Rights would mark its 60th anniversary in 2008 and they could make the declaration 'a living document'.

Here is a remarkable initiative, imaginative and bold in its concept.

Naturally, it remains to be seen whether or not it will achieve the goals the group sets for itself. But there is no doubt that it will make a considerable impact on the world and become a lasting monument to the influence and world stature of Nelson Mandela.

* * *

On the same night as Annan's speech, specially scheduled as one of Mandela's main birthday events, some 35 000 people gathered at the Newlands Rugby Stadium in wintry Cape Town to celebrate Mandela's birthday by watching a spectacularly unusual soccer match between a star-studded World XI and an African XI. It was called the '90 Minutes for Mandela' tribute match and was a fundraiser under the FIFA 'Say No to Racism' banner, regarded as a key Mandela cause. FIFA introduced the anti-racism campaign in 2006 to combat the growing problem of players enduring racist taunts from fans, particularly in Europe, though South African teams have also endured similar slurs.

The day before the kick-off Mandela was presented with the official jersey for the match with his name and the number 89 on the back. It featured his prison number on the front – 46664 – which highlights his campaign to raise global awareness about HIV/AIDS.

Mandela said he was deeply honoured by FIFA's tribute but modestly pointed out that 'it must always be remembered that I was one of many who fought for freedom from tyranny and racism'.

The teams embodied the 'Say No to Racism' theme with the African team wearing white and their opponents black. The match honoured the formation of a soccer league by Robben Island prisoners when Mandela was on the prison island, the Makana Football Association, which adopted FIFA rules. Nelson Mandela watched their games from his prison cell because his jailers did not want him to mix with the players. Later they built a wall to stop him watching.

On the day of the match, FIFA's Vice-President Jack Warner conferred honorary FIFA membership on the club. Thanking FIFA, Nelson Mandela responded in a recorded message broadcast on a giant screen, 'During the dark years of our incarceration, the association drew together all the prisoners on the island around the beautiful game of soccer. In this way it helped uphold the values of inclusiveness and reconciliation, and of non-racialism and peace that are still dear to all of us today.'

He went on, 'This match is more than just a game; it symbolises the power of football to bring people together from all over the world, regardless of the language they speak or the colour of their skin.'

Mandela, known fondly in South Africa by his clan name Madiba, was the magnet that drew in the thousands of spectators even though he did not attend but watched the game at his home in Johannesburg. One among the audience was motor mechanic Johannes Maluleke, from Tzaneen, near Polokwane, nearly 2 000 kilometres away from Cape Town. He gave up going to football stadiums in 1996, 'but this, because it is Mandela's celebration, I could not stay away'. The proceeds from his ticket and that of the others went to the Mandela Foundation and other Mandela charities.

Sixty-six-year-old Brazilian football legend Pele ceremoniously kicked off for the World XI, thirty years after retiring from the sport. He spoke of being honoured to take part in proceedings because he had learnt many life lessons from Mandela. 'We must continue to fight in honour of Mr Mandela against racism and discrimination,' he said.

Liberian George Weah, a former world player of the year also known for his failed bid to become the President of Liberia declared, 'I am a son of Mandela. He has inspired me and fought for our continent. He inspired millions all over the world'; while 45-year-old, former European Player of the Year, Dutch striker Ruud Gullit said the lesson from Mandela's life was that 'there is always hope. If you believe in yourself and fight hard for the right thing, you will succeed.'

The result was a three-goal-all draw.

The next day, another world personage, former United States President Bill Clinton, paid tribute to Mandela. Opening an exhibition commemorating Mandela and former ANC President Chief Albert Luthuli at the Nelson Mandela Foundation offices in Johannesburg, Clinton said that the most important part of Nelson Mandela's legacy was that the world's common humanity matters more than its differences. 'Our differences are wonderful, they make life more interesting, but our common humanity matters more. It is the most important part of his legacy because it's at the heart of every single problem that our children and grandchildren will face.'

Mandela attended the event but did not make a speech.

Clinton said it was important for people across the world to remember and live by the practical implications of Mandela's legacy and not only its spirit. He said he tried to come to South Africa annually around the time of Mandela's birthday. 'I want to see my friend and because he's been the inspiration of much of what I've done.'

The birthday celebrations rolled on into another party on Tuesday, 24 July at the Nelson Mandela Children's Fund offices in Johannesburg where a beaming Mandela cut a huge birthday cake, gave hugs and received gifts at his annual children's party. At his side was Graça Machel.

The good wishes were spelled out by many of the 300 children in frequently exotic language. One called him 'the angel of heaven'; five-year-old Robert wrote, 'You are the goodest man in the world'; Franco, four, said Mandela was 'the boss of the whole country', while Olerato, five, said, 'You are the best man ever'.

Zolile Cele, eleven, gave Madiba a folding chair made by fellow pupils at the special needs Forest Town school in Johannesburg. Speaking from his wheelchair, he said meeting Nelson Mandela was 'cool'; he was 'something big to me'.

'When Mr Mandela sees children, he just melts. He holds them very dear to his heart,' comments Tumi Mdwaba, spokeswoman for the Nelson Mandela Children's Fund.

*　*　*

Who is this man who inspires so many? Advocate George Bizos, who has known Mandela for nearly half a century and defended him at the Rivonia Trial in the early 1960s, which resulted in Mandela's 27 years of imprisonment, describes him in those days as 'tall, handsome, well dressed, self confident, a "volunteer-in-chief" taking part in the Defiance Campaign, making speeches in Alexandra Township and in Freedom Square in Soweto'.

Bizos spoke at length about his association with Mandela when he was featured by e-TV's Debora Patta in her *Third Degree* programme on 5 June 2007. Said Bizos, 'He was a person whom you would respect as an individual and be impressed by his very presence. He was known to be a leader of the ANC Youth League.'

Debora Patta noted that Bizos in his book *Odyssey to Freedom*, had described Mandela 'as never resting; he would wear his suit all day long and he was always busy even with the common law prisoners', adding that that conduct continued right throughout his imprisonment.

'Absolutely!' replied Bizos. 'He symbolised the unity of the oppressed people that "we can't afford to have differences between us which the younger people, in particular, were concerned (about) and argued over".'

Bizos made a telling point about the conduct of the apartheid government. 'They thought that if they isolated political prisoners on Robben Island that would destroy the movement. They were so wrong. They really opened the school for freedom fighters because once they had served their term they came out, inculcated by Mandela's ideas and leadership and it was counter-productive for the authorities.'

Debora Patta asked him, 'What do you value most about your friendship with Mandela?'

Bizos replied:

Well, he showed me the way in many respects. His optimism that one day all the people of South Africa would be free, even us whites that we would be freed from the prejudices that we tended to have. His loyalty to friendship, to common people who made sacrifices as he did and his absolute belief that there would be freedom in his lifetime.

Bizos, already well-known as a defender of the downtrodden in apartheid abuses, became famous as part of the team that included the Afrikaner

Bram Fischer – a descendant of an Orange Free State Boer President – that defended Mandela in one of the most important court cases of the twentieth century, the Rivonia Trial.

Patta reminded Bizos that he is 'widely credited for saving Mandela and his colleagues from the death penalty', and Bizos answered modestly, 'I am given too much credit.'

He explained that his concern arose from the content of the historic statement Nelson Mandela made before sentence was passed. He was worried that the wording might have influenced the judge to give greater consideration to the death penalty.

Bizos commented:

My only contribution to it (the statement) is that when the almost final draft was produced, I was disturbed by his statement that he was prepared to die for what he believed in.

And I engaged him in conversation and I said, 'You know, Nelson, that this may be misinterpreted that you are seeking martyrdom. You surely want to live and to enjoy what you stand for and want to come about. Surely, that is what you should say.' And he worked on the final paragraph but he took my advice to say 'and if needs be, for which I am prepared to die'. That's all my contribution was.

As it was eventually delivered in calm, slow, measured tones, Mandela's statement from the dock sounded through the courtroom:

I have fought against white domination and I have fought against black domination. I have cherished the idea of a democratic and free society in which all persons live together in harmony and with equal opportunities. It is an idea for which I hope to live for and to see realised, but, my Lord, if it needs be, it is an idea for which I am prepared to die.[1]

Patta asked, 'Were you gutted when they got life?'

And Bizos replied, 'That's strange. It was a relief. Of course, life imprisonment is not a sentence to be happy about. But we were all optimistic that they would not serve it.'

In the event most of them did serve a life term.

Bizos summed up his views of Nelson Mandela and the other freedom fighters he was in contact with in a telling assessment in which he submerged himself into the background. Asked what he is most proud of, he said:

with having made some contribution in having crossed their path; they are the heroes. Lawyers play a secondary role. In order to be a good lawyer you need good clients and I have been fortunate to have crossed the path of great men, brave men, unselfish men and women who were prepared to

Nelson and Winnie greet supporters.

Maki Mohale, Mary Mxadana and Mandela celebrate the results of the election.

forsake their freedom, prepared to offer their lives for the sake of freedom. And the fact that I was allowed to play a secondary role in their lives is something that I am very proud of.

President Thabo Mbeki, who wished Nelson Mandela happy birthday on behalf of the government and people of South Africa, said the country and the world were privileged to celebrate the life of such 'an outstanding leader of our people'. Former President Mandela inspired South Africa, the continent and the rest of humanity through his life, his leadership and his resolute and deep-seated commitment to the struggle against apartheid and for a just and democratic society, said Mbeki.

Mandela's popularity is legendary and, according to a May 2007 survey conducted by the Markinor research company, he is becoming more popular with age. On his 89th birthday, in a survey of 3 500 people representing South Africa's adult population, Nelson Mandela scored an average rating of 9.2 out of 10, making him the country's most beloved leader.

But just when Mandela is at the pinnacle of popular acclaim, he and the Nelson Mandela Foundation are busy trying to 'demythologise' or, put more crudely, to 'rebrand' him. The Foundation has asked for public input as to how this could be done.

Foundation staff have come up with the idea of removing the image of Mandela's face from their publications and replacing it with an image of his outstretched left hand with the wedding band prominently displayed.

Although it appears that Nelson Mandela is the moving spirit behind the project the reasons for wanting to do this are unclear. At least one newspaper columnist, William Saunderson-Meyer, has reacted with surprise and is trying to understand the reason for what he terms this 'bizarre' intention. Saunderson-Meyer comments:

The Foundation's intentions are all a bit fuzzy. A successful symbol is not some kind of Rorschach inkblot test, into which you read whatever you happen to be feeling at that moment. The best symbols are consistent, unambiguous embodiments of qualities, values and aspirations. Mandela, himself, understands this well. It was his crucial intervention that saved the Springbok as the century-old symbol of South African rugby, when the African National Congress took power in 1994.[2]

It is difficult to know why the Foundation wants to interfere with the success of the Mandela phenomenon. Perhaps God and Muhammad need some judicious market repositioning – a bit of tweaking here and there to draw support in a critical, fickle world. But is that necessary for Mandela?

This is a man whom the whole world adores and has elevated to the status of its first secular saint. A United States branding survey a few years back valued the Mandela brand as second only to Coca-Cola internationally. Coke spends billions to build and safeguard its brand. Mandela simply goes around being himself.

Raymond Louw was born in Cape Town, South Africa. He started his journalism career on the *Rand Daily Mail* in Johannesburg and is a veteran campaigner for media freedom issues. Louw is currently the editor and publisher of *Southern Africa Report*, a weekly current affairs newsletter.

Notes

1. Mandela's statement from the dock was replayed in the course of the *Third Degree* interview with George Bizos.

2. William Saunderson-Meyer, 'Secular Saint to get a Makeover', *Jaundiced Eye*, 23 July 2007.

GENEROSITY OF SPIRIT

Benjamin Pogrund

At the end of the 1950s, Nelson Mandela was a deeply committed leader in the ANC. He had been one of the moving forces in the ANC's Youth League which had set the organisation on the road to modernity and confrontation with the apartheid government in bringing about a change in the national leadership in 1949; he had been the volunteer-in-chief of the Defiance Campaign in 1952, and had been elected leader in the Transvaal province – and been forced out of it by government banning orders; since December 1956 he had been one of the accused in the ongoing Treason Trial.

Despite all this, a playboy image clung to Mandela. He wasn't quite serious about his politics was the whisper in some ANC circles. He was different from other leaders: tall, well-built and handsome, he dressed well, he had a reputation for enjoying socialising, he drove a car, and his wife, in his second marriage, was the beautiful and glamorous Winnie. And, of course, he had unusual status as one of the few black people who had qualified as an attorney.

As the years were to prove, the imagined image could not possibly have been further from the truth. Mandela knowingly and willingly put himself into the cauldron of political involvement at a time when white power was total and heavy penalties awaited any black person who resisted or who even dared to talk back.

Mandela had already had a taste of that in the magistrates' courts in which he practised together with his ANC colleague, Oliver Tambo. Their firm occupied a few offices in Chancellor House across the street from the large courts building in Fox Street, Johannesburg, and around the corner from the basement offices of the ANC. Appearing before the magistrates, all of whom were white, was not easy. The magistrates generally were at best uncomfortable, at worst hostile, at having to deal with a black lawyer. They had to observe the forms of courtesy in their courts, but it was plain that some did not like having to treat a black man with politeness and as an equal in law. Mandela, when he appeared before them, was courteous but made plain that he was standing his ground.

I saw him at work in the courts in the aftermath of the women's protests against the pass laws in 1959. The requirement that blacks had to carry a pass at all times or face instant arrest was being extended to women: thousands were arrested for expressing their determined opposition. I was a young journalist on the *Rand Daily Mail* newspaper learning the trade as a reporter at the magistrates' courts. I already knew Mandela and he told me that mass trials of arrested women were being held in the basement of the building where the holding cells were situated, and that the press was excluded from the hearings. This, he and I agreed, was wrong in law. I went to see the chief magistrate and complained, threatening an application to the Supreme Court. The hearings were immediately opened to the press. From then on, over the next six weeks, I sat in on the trials with Mandela among the lawyers who fought to get the women acquitted or at least get them the lightest possible sentences.

A decade later, when Mandela was a prisoner on Robben Island, he wrote me a letter. Believing, probably rightly, that the authorities would not let it go through, he addressed it to someone else. The clue to the intended recipient was hidden in the contents of the letter because he referred to what had occurred in forcing the opening of the magistrates' court cells to the press. The letter was passed from one person to another as they tried to figure out who it was meant for, finally reaching me after several months.

The anti-pass protests were part of the turmoil of that era. Laws to enforce apartheid were pouring out of the all-white parliament and the ANC struggled to resist. It was not successful. The Pan-Africanist Congress (PAC) emerged as a rival organisation and set the pace for resistance by calling on blacks to leave their passes at home and go to their nearest police station to offer themselves for arrest. The campaign was launched on 21 March 1960 and the results are history: the popular response was patchy but in the township of Sharpeville, near Vereeniging, where a peaceful crowd of thousands did gather, police opened fire and killed 68 people. That galvanised the ANC and it called for protests a week later. As insurrection flared around the country, the government banned both the ANC and the PAC, declared a State of Emergency and detained thousands without trial.

The events put new steel into Mandela. With Tambo going into exile abroad, Mandela increasingly became the primary leader. He grew into the role and was the dominant force in driving ahead the next year to express black opposition to the intention of the Afrikaner Nationalists to fulfil their long-cherished dream of declaring a republic, harking back

Orlando East, Soweto.

to the Boer republics which had been swept away by the South African War at the turn of the twentieth century. Mandela created the All-in African National Action Council, a thinly disguised version of the banned ANC. He persuaded a wider section of blacks to take part in it by calling for a general strike on Monday 29 May 1961. It was illegal for black workers to strike so it was called a 'stay-at-home'.

The protest's formal launch took place in Pietermaritzburg in March. It was a standard ANC mass gathering: speaker after speaker and with a pre-arranged set of resolutions to be endorsed by popular vote. Excitement swept through the crowded hall when Mandela was suddenly introduced as a speaker. His name was known, although he had been little seen at meetings around the country for much of the previous nine years. He had been under intermittent bannings which prohibited him from attending meetings or social gatherings, which meant he could not be with more than two people at a time; and he was confined to Johannes-

burg (except for being allowed to go to Pretoria for the Treason Trial). Despite these restrictions Mandela was highly active inside the ANC. When government bannings had commenced at the start of the 1950s, the ANC had decided on a policy of 'We stand by our leaders', with the result that banned leaders continued to work in secret. The reason for this was laudable but it did mean that a leadership developed which was never subjected to open election and which gradually lost touch with the rank and file because it could not be in easy contact with people.

The best and the worst of this was in evidence in Pietermaritzburg. The Mandela name was known, but the person wasn't. His latest bannings had expired a short while before and he made a surprise appearance on the platform: the announcement of his name as a speaker was greeted with great applause, but he was also a stranger. In later years, it was claimed that Mandela made a colossal impression at that meeting. But he did not. He delivered a formulaic speech and left quickly out of a

16 June 1976, youth celebrate after receiving permission to march by the police.

side door before the Security Police outside the hall probably even knew he was there. The meeting went on to endorse the protest call.

Mandela's charisma seldom reveals itself in set speeches. But his power and ability to reach out to people and enfold them comes when he speaks without notes. The phrases might have been pre-prepared and for someone who went on to make as many speeches as he did, frequent repetition of thoughts and phrases was inevitable. But the homely, human quality comes through. Anyone who has heard him knows it, such as at an event in Britain in the mid-1990s, when Mandela made an early visit as President of the new South Africa and spoke to a crowd of many hundreds in the garden of the home of the first post-apartheid High Commissioner, Mendi Msimang. The crowd consisted of expatriates, chiefly whites; they were talented South Africans who had emigrated over the years. Mandela spoke to them of coming home, of how they were needed to build the new South Africa. His words and thoughts were direct and personal, with shafts of the self-deprecating humour which is his style. I watched the reactions of people around me: he had them in the palm of his hand. He spoke for about twenty minutes and I had no doubt that if, at the end, he had announced that a fleet of aircraft was waiting at Heathrow airport to carry them back, there would have been a mass rush to get on board.

* * *

In declaring his intention to disrupt the May 1961 Republic Day celebrations, Mandela made himself a target for government attack. But first they had to find him and this became a top priority for the police. They scoured the country but Mandela eluded them and became known as the 'Black Pimpernel', after the famous Baroness Orczy fictional character. Yet he did not resort to any great disguises. He was sheltered by supporters and held meetings in secret to further the stay-at-home. As a reporter who was by now specialising in black politics, I was seeing him whenever I wanted to, or whenever he wanted to speak to me. The only other reporter with this access was the late Charles Bloomberg of the *Sunday Times*, who later left the country because of his justifiable fear of the consequences after writing a report exposing the Afrikaner Broederbond, the sinister organisation which pulled government strings from behind the scenes.

Mandela and I sent messages to each other when either of us wanted to meet. The regular venue was the home in the suburb of Fordsburg of Adelaide and Paul Joseph, members of the Transvaal Indian Congress. Or else we met at night in a quiet street nearby: I would park in a dark spot and he would appear. His only disguise was to wear worker's overalls, which did nothing to conceal his imposing presence. We sat in my car and talked about what he was doing. To ensure a flow of news for publication, we arranged that I would be at my desk at the *Mail* at 5:00 p.m. each day. Whenever necessary, a phone call would come in and a voice would read an Action Council statement to me. It was never Mandela, but others who phoned, and sometimes I recognised the voice of a friend.

Again, the history is that the protest failed. Government intimidation and show of force and threats did the job. South Africa went onto a new track. My personal memory of Mandela is of two of his responses at the time. The first came on the morning of the strike: the *Rand Daily Mail* rushed out a special edition to get to the streets by 8:00 a.m. The strike was not a success; nor was it a total failure. Perhaps 50 per cent of workers responded. But the *Mail*, in its haste, accepted the word of government and municipal officials, and declared that the strike had flopped. The *Mail* was viewed with such respect by blacks that its banner headline ended whatever hope the strike might yet have had of succeeding. I was sitting at my desk, feeling miserable and angry over what we had done when Mandela phoned. I began to stutter an apology but he cut me off and said he knew it was not my fault. I was overwhelmed by the generosity of spirit from a man who had spent months putting his life on the line for his cause, who had sacrificed family and career for it, and yet who now evinced not a hint of bitterness or despair.

When he phoned again that night, I was profoundly impressed by his honesty. There was no attempt to gloss over what had happened or to put a spin on events in the way that politicians usually did. Instead he said to me frankly, 'The people did not respond to the stay-at-home to the extent to which we expected them to do.' He went on to say, 'We are not disheartened. This is not the end of the matter …' An hour later he phoned again, apparently in response to the questions I had put to him about his future intentions, and gave the first fateful announcement of a switch to armed resistance. He spoke of the 'closing of a chapter' and said, 'I don't think, speaking for myself, that I can continue speak-

ing peace and non-violence in the light of the methods adopted by the government to suppress our peaceful protest …'

* * *

My family has had personal experience of Mandela's kindness. In January 1986, my son, Gideon, was celebrating his bar mitzvah, the Jewish rite of passage to manhood at the age of thirteen. I had visited Mandela at Pollsmoor prison a few weeks earlier and told him about it. He must have gone to some trouble to get hold of quality paper and he wrote a note of good wishes to Gideon. Four years later, when Mandela was released from prison, I phoned him from London where we were living. After welcoming him to freedom I gave the phone to Gideon who started by saying 'Hello Mr Mandela' – and back came the deep, booming voice, 'What's this Mr Mandela? Call me Uncle Nelson.' It left Gideon with stars in his eyes.

Later, Mandela went out of his way to help my daughter Jennifer. He enabled her to join him on African presidential planes when, in 1991, he visited West Africa for the first time in thirty years. Then he had been seeking support for the ANC after slipping out of South Africa. Now he had iconic status and was greeted rapturously. She produced and directed a documentary about his visit, 'The Last Mile: Mandela, Africa and Democracy'. One scene showed him on Goree Island, off the coast of Dakar, from where millions of slaves had been shipped to the Americas; and it also contained relaxed and personal moments as he talked about his life and his hopes for the democracy-to-come in South Africa.

* * *

The late Piet Beyleveld was a leader in the Springbok Legion, the organisation of Second World War ex-servicemen which was taken over by communists. He was later president of the Congress of Democrats, the communist front group for whites set up as part of the Congress Alliance with the ANC. Beyleveld was an amiable fellow, honest and well-intentioned in his opposition to apartheid. The Security Police detained him and he turned against his former comrades: he admitted he had been a member of the party since 1956 and became a witness for the prosecution to get them jailed.

Some time afterwards I went to talk to him. He spoke freely and described the last secret party conference he had attended, in a house in Johannesburg, early in the 1960s. He offered the information that Mandela had been there and, he believed, had even been elected to membership of the central committee. He said the balloting was secret and the committee's names were not supposed to be known even in party circles.

At the time, this information was dynamite. The government was

President Thabo Mbeki at the 95th anniversary of the ANC in Witbank, 2007.

desperate to prove that Mandela was or had been a communist. But I did not report Beyleveld's information and instead locked it away in my mind: I did not know to what extent the Security Police had turned him into a cat's paw and I was determined not to let them use me to smear Mandela. The story remained a puzzle. Then, in 2007, Padraig O'Malley, in his biography of Mac Maharaj, who was jailed with Mandela, quotes party members as saying that Mandela, for a short time, was indeed a member. So it turns out, more than forty years later, that Piet Beyleveld told me the truth.

* * *

In mid-1961, ANC leaders met in secret and took the fateful decision to create Umkhonto we Sizwe (MK), the Spear of the Nation, to wage armed struggle against apartheid. Mandela was put in charge. The decision had a crucial proviso – attacks would be made on property, and there would not be any killing of civilians. This was based firstly on the ANC's belief in Mahatma Gandhi's policy of non-violence and secondly on the strategic view that killing whites would serve only to reinforce their fear of majority rule. With only a few exceptions this policy was maintained for the next three decades. With the new policy in place, Mandela travelled through Africa and went to Britain and the Soviet Union.

The government was on guard for his return but he slipped back without being intercepted, coming in from the then Bechuanaland, now Botswana. The British colonial authorities there knew the exact moment and place of his entry into South Africa, but did not tell Pretoria. I was told this by the security chief, Gerry Forrest, and believed him because I knew from previous interviews that he had a low opinion of the South African police and disliked his security counterparts because of their ideological zealotry. One incident which had irritated him was when he drove to South Africa and a policeman at the border ordered him to open the bonnet of his car. 'Do you think I am hiding Mandela in the engine?' Forrest had asked sarcastically.

In August 1962, Mandela was captured while travelling in Natal, and was tried and jailed for incitement and leaving the country illegally. Later, while imprisoned, the Rivonia raid took place and, using documentary evidence found there, he and other colleagues were put on trial on the far graver charges of seeking to overthrow the government by force. The death penalty was a heavy cloud over the trial and was feared as a real possibility. Outside government circles it was thought at the time that it was only the strength of international pressures which caused the judge to draw back and instead impose life imprisonment on Mandela.

– * * *

Mandela was taken to Robben Island maximum-security prison as one of the 1 400 or so prisoners held there. The government refused to acknowledge them as political prisoners and insisted that they receive the same level of imprisonment as ordinary criminal prisoners (except that the political prisoners were denied the virtually automatic one-third remission of sentence given to murderers, rapists and robbers). Mandela had the lesser standards of food assigned to blacks compared with his coloured and Asian fellow-prisoners – and they all had even less than the whites, also jailed in the Rivonia Trial, who were kept at Pretoria Local prison.

The *Rand Daily Mail* helped to improve life for Mandela and other black prisoners through our exposé of poor prison conditions in 1965. The government denied the truth of what we published and spent the next four years prosecuting our informants and finally the editor and myself as the reporter; however, at the same time, it acted to improve conditions. A particular result for Mandela and others, relieving their winter misery in the cold concrete cells, was that they were given shoes and socks instead of rubber sandals (some prisoners didn't even have these but went barefoot); they were given long trousers instead of three-quarter-length 'tsotsi' ('gangster') shorts, and had jerseys as a matter of course. The harsh conditions gradually eased and there was an end to the warders' brutality to which Mandela was at first subjected.

Mandela continued to grow as a person. His natural charisma and leadership qualities came to the fore. Not only did he lead the ANC men in the prison, but he was also respected by the ANC's political rivals – the Pan-Africanists and their Poqo offshoots, the small African Resistance Movement and the smaller Yu Chi Chan Club. Mandela was always available to give advice to anyone who wanted it. He was known for his calmness and willingness to listen to what others had to say.

For the country's ruling whites he was a forgotten figure. This was also the case in the rest of the world: in the year of the first Rivonia Trial the *New York Times* published about a dozen reports in which the Mandela name featured; the next year, it appeared only once, and that was with regard to Winnie Mandela. She went on courageously working to keep his name and cause alive, and in doing so incurred the hatred of the Security Police. At some stage, a decision was seemingly taken by the

Congress Alliance leaders abroad to focus public attention on Mandela: his strengths were recognised and made him a desirable icon.

It took time but gradually his name came to the forefront and came to symbolise the anti-apartheid struggle. This showed itself in strange little ways: on a summer's Saturday afternoon I drove to the Central Post Office in Johannesburg to send a registered letter to Mandela in prison. A black man was the counter clerk. He was tired and hot and sprawled across the counter, his head resting on his arm. I handed the letter to him, he gave it a bored look – but, as he saw the name, he came alive in an instant. He sat up, his eyes shining, and gave me impeccable service.

* * *

During the 1970s and early 1980s the apartheid government began to wake up to Mandela's importance as a leader. As he grew older the government feared he would die in prison and become a martyr figure to rally worldwide opposition to apartheid. Overtures were made to him for his release by his nephew, Paramount Chief Kaiser Matanzima, and Johan Coetzee of the Security Police. The condition was that Mandela had to agree to leave South Africa itself and live in the Transkei, the so-called independent bantustan headed by Matanzima. Mandela refused.

Mandela and five of his closest colleagues were transferred from Robben Island to the easier conditions of Pollsmoor prison on the mainland. From early in 1985, cabinet ministers began to visit him for secret meetings and he was taken to see President P.W. Botha. After years of making written applications I was finally allowed to visit him for 45 minutes. I was told I was being allowed to see him as a friend, not as a journalist, and had to promise I would not write about it. That was hard for me, and I also had to get my *Rand Daily Mail* colleagues to accept it.

I had already got to know Mandela's security warder, Warrant Officer James Gregory. Over the years, starting with Robben Island, my wife, Anne, and I had sent parcels of food delicacies for Mandela at Christmas time. Then, one year, I was told it would have to be shared with every prisoner on the Island. I phoned prison headquarters and an officer confirmed this.

'Do you mean that if I send one kilogram of sweets you will distribute them among 1 400 prisoners?' I asked.

'Yes,' was the answer. That was clearly absurd but instead, from then on, we were allowed to send money which was credited to Mandela's prison account. In time, we did the same for Mandela's colleagues, Walter Sisulu and Govan Mbeki. I was told that, at Christmas, they could write lists of the food they wanted and warders would go to the nearest supermarket to do the buying.

On our annual holiday in Cape Town we drove to Pollsmoor prison to leave gifts. I dealt with Gregory and he was always polite and helpful.

At home in Johannesburg one Saturday morning, Winnie phoned in a state of distress: she had been told that Mandela had cancer and wanted me to attempt to verify the rumour immediately. I phoned Pollsmoor and got hold of Gregory. He assured me there was no truth in it; he had seen Mandela only a short time before and he was well and had had a good breakfast. Gregory asked me to tell this to Winnie, and added how terrible it was that there were people who spread rumours like this. I thanked him and asked him please to convey my best wishes to Mr Mandela and he said he would do so. It was surreal and hard to believe I was talking to a warder about the country's No. 1 prisoner. I put down the phone and said to Anne, 'That is one of the maddest phone conversations I have ever had.'

In preparing to visit Mandela I made up my mind that I would say whatever I wanted and would not allow any censorship. I was admitted to Pollsmoor prison and was welcomed by Gregory: he said how excited they all were by the visit. I suddenly realised mine was a trial visit – the authorities wanted to see what happened because for many years only family members had been allowed to see Mandela. I panicked and blurted out that of course I would go along with whatever the rules might be. Don't worry, said Gregory; the 'Old Man' knew what was allowed and we were not allowed to talk about prison conditions.

It was a special moment in my life: I sat on a stool in front of a large sheet of glass and in walked Nelson Mandela, his hands held high and calling out a greeting. He sat on the other side of the glass and we spoke though loudspeakers, giving our voices a disembodied tone. He was grey-haired and his face was lined. But he held himself erect and he looked as robust as when I had last seen him, more than two decades before. I was struck by his gravitas. This was a man who had endured and had become serious and deeper in the process. He spoke with authority. He was polite to Gregory and Gregory was polite to him, but Mandela, prisoner though he was, was the man in charge.

He had prepared a list of topics for our meeting: he wanted me to help clear the way for the education of two of his daughters, and he wanted to know about a range of old friends. He asked me to tell Dr Harold Seftel, an expert in African medicine, whom he had known when they were students at the University of the Witwatersrand, that he listened to his daily health talk on the radio. I had to tell Seftel that Mandela was following his advice and had cut down on his salt intake. It was a small world because not only did I know Harry Seftel, but his sister, Dolly Levine, was a close friend who had introduced Anne and I – a 'shidduch' in Yiddish – and she maintained a proprietary interest in our marriage and children. Later, I phoned Seftel with Mandela's message and he excitedly thanked me, 'It's a mitzvah [blessing] you are giving me, it's a mitzvah.'

Mandela asked me to visit again, for double the time, but said he would not see me unless Anne came along too. They had never met – we

married after his imprisonment – but he said he had a photograph of her on his cell wall. Anne and I did visit, in January 1986, a few weeks before emigrating to Britain, and this time Mandela's authority was even more marked. We had a contact visit in an office and the prisons colonel who sat behind the desk taking notes was clearly only formally in charge. This time I had to give a written undertaking in advance that I would not write about the visit.

*   *   *

The South African government announced on a Friday that Mandela was to be released the next day. On the Saturday, I had to attend to the repair of a chair at a small antique shop near our home in West Hampstead, London. I walked in and said cheerfully to the owner, 'Wonderful news that Nelson Mandela is being released today.' He spat back at me, 'He's a terrorist. He should be strung up.' It was an ugly moment but did not reflect British popular opinion of the time. I spent the rest of the day at Sky TV, providing a running commentary on the amazing images beamed from outside the Victor Verster prison in the countryside and then from Cape Town's Grand Parade where Mandela spoke to a crowd of many thousands.

*   *   *

Among the many, many wonderful stories about Mandela my favourite is the one told to me by Jules Browde, the well-known Johannesburg white lawyer who defended people in political trials in the apartheid era. Years ago I used the story in a small book about Mandela meant for high school students. Browde recalls telling Mandela that he and his wife were going out one night and their son of four was being left with a black nanny and cried, 'I don't want to be left with a black face.' Browde told Mandela he could not understand it, 'We are liberal people and there is no trace of racism in our home.' Mandela said he had the same problem at home, in reverse: white friends had recently visited and when they left his child had said, 'Why do you have white people here?' Mandela said he replied, 'Not all white people have white hearts. Some have black hearts.'

*   *   *

Benjamin Pogrund was born in Cape Town, South Africa. In 1958 he joined the *Rand Daily Mail* in Johannesburg and pioneered the reporting of black politics and existence under apartheid. He was deputy editor when the newspaper was closed down in 1985 and he emigrated to Britain. He currently lives in Jerusalem where he is the Director of Yakar's Center for Social Concern.

THE EARLY YEARS

PREVIOUS PAGE: *A pass book: the chain that shackled the lives and movements of black South Africans.*

ABOVE: *Pass offenders: these men were arrested for not carrying their pass books.*

ABOVE RIGHT: *Police chase women demonstrators down the streets of Johannesburg in 1958.*
The women were protesting against the issuing of pass books to men, women and children.

BELOW RIGHT: *A woman argues with police at a demonstration against the carrying of pass books.*

FOLLOWING PAGE: *'Europeans only': a young girl with her nanny in 1956.*

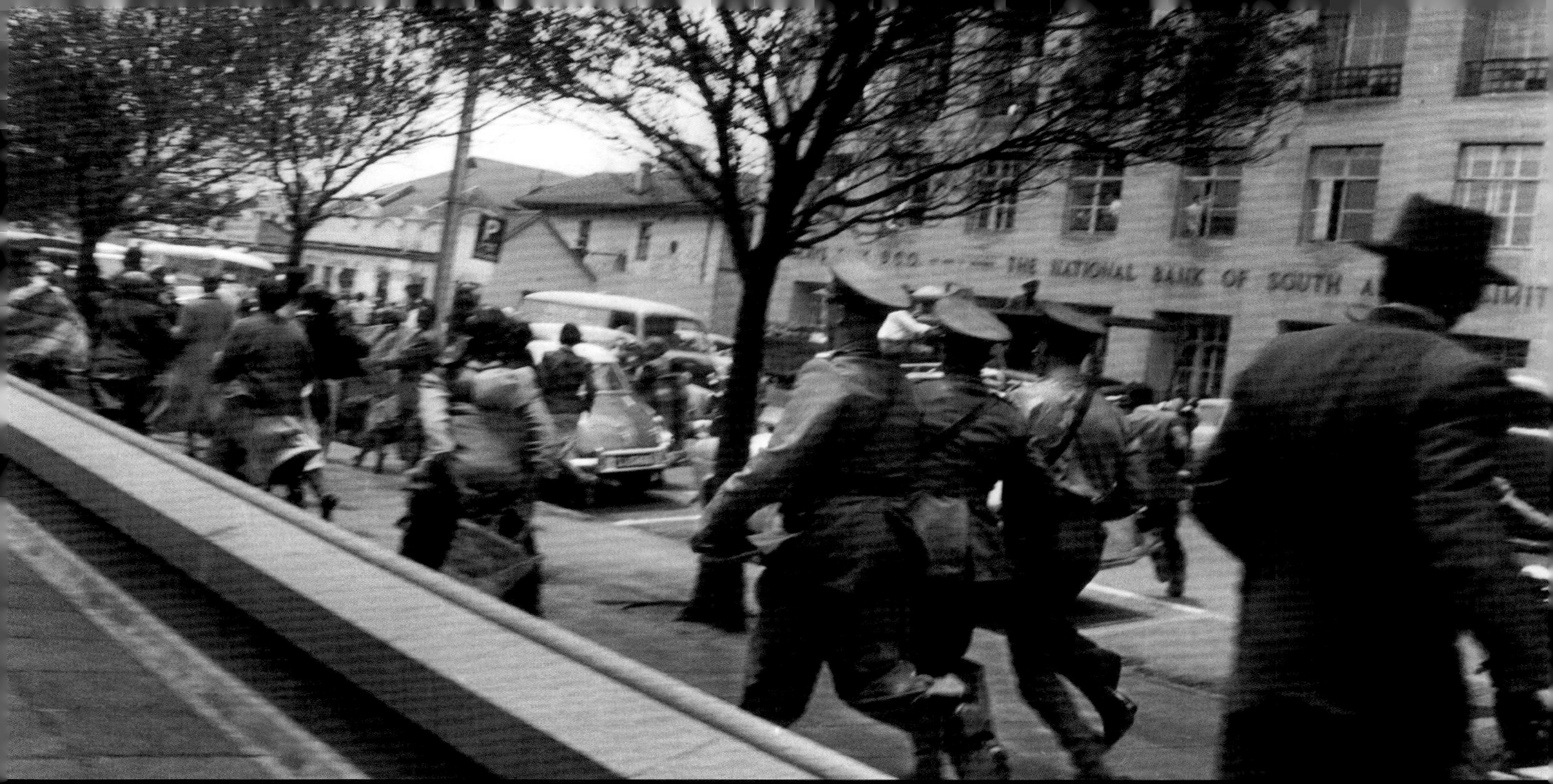
THE NATIONAL BANK OF SOUTH

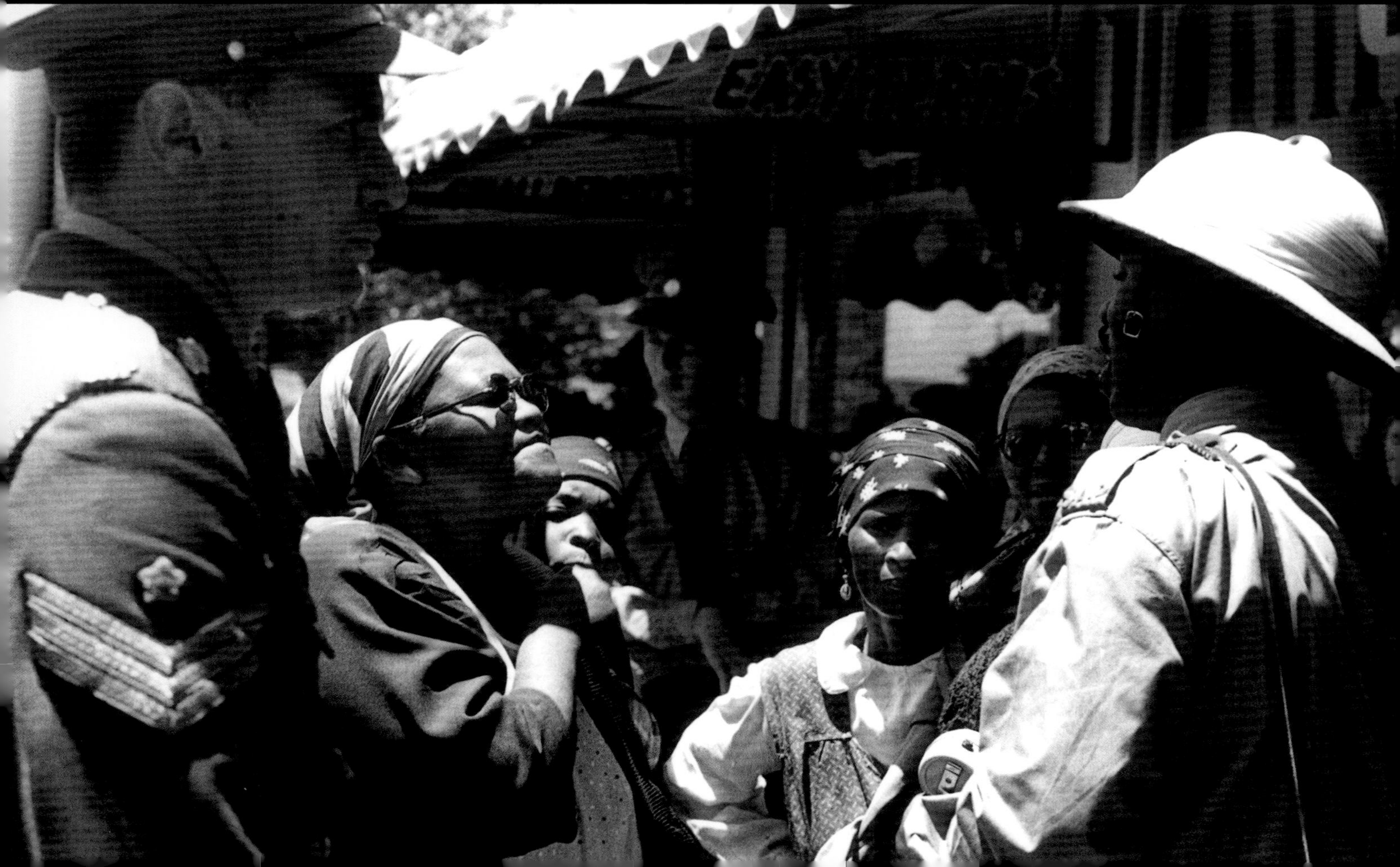

The forced removal of people from
Sophiatown to Meadowlands, Soweto.

LEFT: *Nelson Mandela addresses a group of women during their march to Pretoria's Union Buildings to protest against the pass laws. These laws forced all Africans over the age of sixteen to carry pass books. Failure to do so could mean arrest, a jail sentence or a fine.*

ABOVE: *Mandela with Peter Nthite, a Youth League leader.*

FOLLOWING PAGE: *ANC members and sympathisers gather outside the Drill Hall in support of the Treason trialists.*

LEFT: *Three of the Treason Trial defendants – (left to right) Robert Resha, Patrick Molaoa and Nelson Mandela – arrive in Pretoria in August 1958.*

ABOVE: *Supporters join Mandela in song outside the court in 1958.*

ABOVE: *Mandela conversing with fellow activist Ruth First, the wife of Joe Slovo who was the Secretary-General of the Communist Party of South Africa.*

ABOVE RIGHT: *Mandela greets well-wishers outside the Pretoria Synagogue.*

ABOVE FAR RIGHT: *Victorious: Advocate Issy Maisels on the shoulders of the acquitted Treason trialists, March 1961.*

BELOW RIGHT: *Bus 638 returns from the Pretoria Synagogue empty: the Treason trialists were all acquitted.*

Would-be miners humiliated by being forced to strip naked for tuberculosis X-rays.

LEFT: *Inside a mine recruiting centre in Eloff Street, Johannesburg, in 1957. This toilet seated sixteen people at a time.*

ABOVE: *The stark conditions of a miners' single-sex dormitory.*

TOP: *The bodies of a child and man killed in the Sharpeville massacre.*

ABOVE: *Stretching into the distance are the coffins of the people massacred in Sharpeville on 21 March 1960.*

RIGHT: *Mourners help with the graves of those killed in the Sharpeville massacre.*

Supporters outside the Pretoria Supreme Court at the Rivonia Trial in 1964.

ABOVE: *Nelson and Winnie's daughters, Zenani and Zindziswa (known as Zindzi), with a friend at their home, No. 8115 Orlando West, Soweto.*

RIGHT: *Winnie Mandela behind the wheel of her Fiat in 1964.*

LEFT: *Winnie with her younger sister, Nonyaniso, and girls, Zenani and Zindzi, on her return from detention.*

RIGHT: *Winnie with her young daughters, Zenani and Zindzi.*

ABOVE RIGHT: *Winnie with Fikile and Vusi Magubane and Zindzi and Zenani in 1971.*

BELOW RIGHT: *Zenani Mandela's fifth birthday party, with Zindzi and Fikile Magubane on her right.*

ABOVE: *Winnie and Zindzi in Brandfort on the first day of Winnie's banishment there in 1977.*
After a few years, she defied her banning order and returned to her home in Soweto.

LEFT: *Zindzi Mandela dressed in traditional attire as a young girl.*

ABOVE: *'Government property' in physical location only: Winnie Mandela outside her house while banished in Brandfort.*

A STRUGGLE
WITHOUT DOCUMENTATION
IS NO STRUGGLE

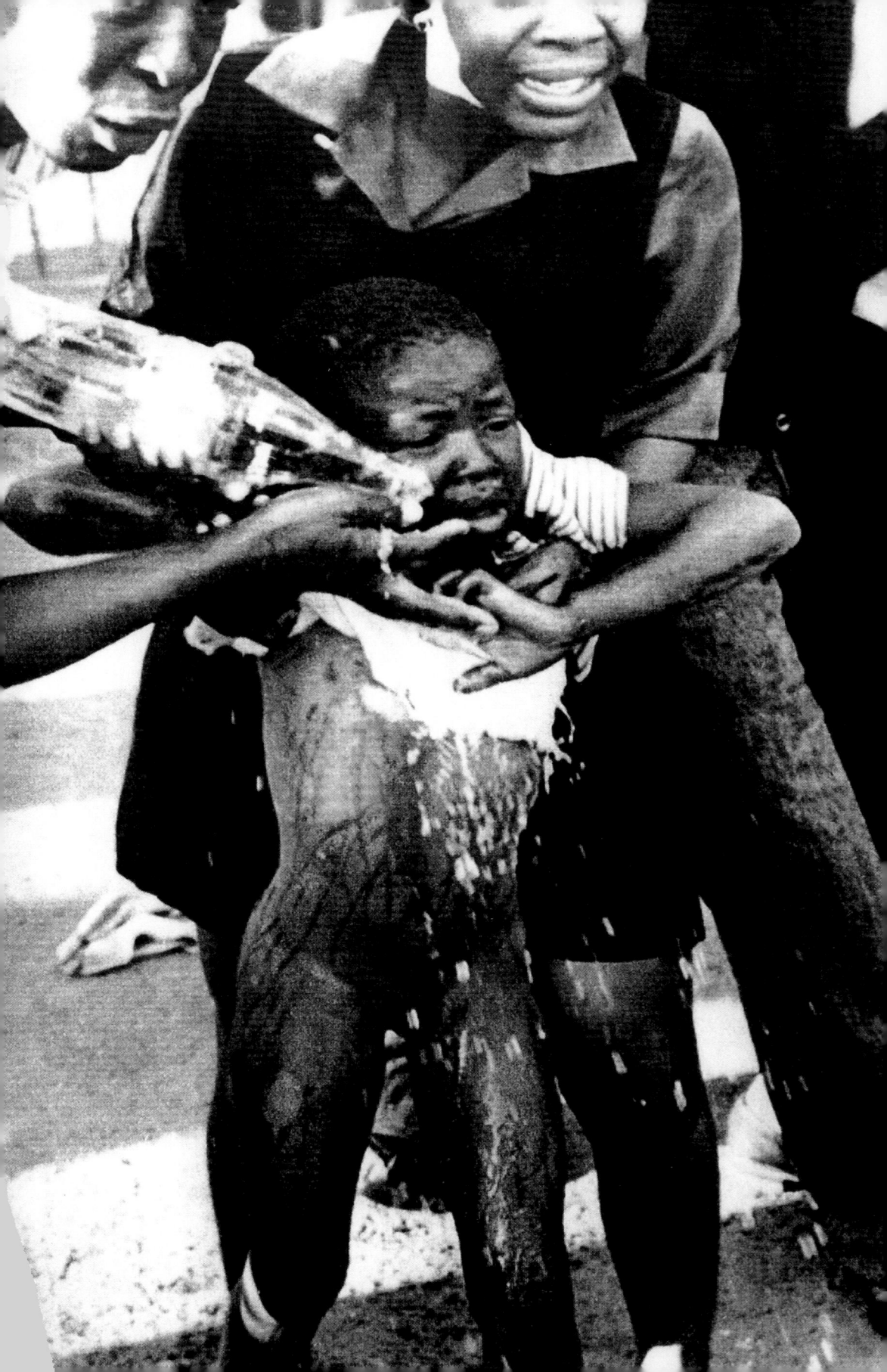

SECTION OPENING: *Newspapers were used to cover the dead in the wake of the uprising in Soweto on 16 June 1976.*

PREVIOUS PAGE: *The first day of the Soweto uprising, 16 June 1976. Smiling children begin their peaceful march unaware of what lay ahead. Peter Magubane met the protesting students who did not want to be photographed. Peter said to them, 'A struggle without documentation is no struggle.' He was then allowed to take these pictures of an event that was to change the course of South Africa's history.*

LEFT: *A little girl falls victim to police teargas.*

ABOVE: *Fighting bullets with stones in Alexandra, 17 June 1976. This young boy was hit by a police bullet seconds after this photograph was taken.*

ABOVE: *A young woman's stomach is sliced open by a police bullet in Alexandra Township on 17 June 1976.*

RIGHT: *Soweto on fire, Meadowlands, June 1976.*

LEFT: *Youths flee police in Alexandra Township on 17 June 1976.*

ABOVE: *Teargas in Soweto.*

FOLLOWING PAGE: *More innocent fall: the coffin of a two-year-old child who was killed by a policeman is carried during a funeral in Mamelodi.*

Students at the University of Cape Town take part in one of the many 'Release Mandela' campaigns held during the 1980s.

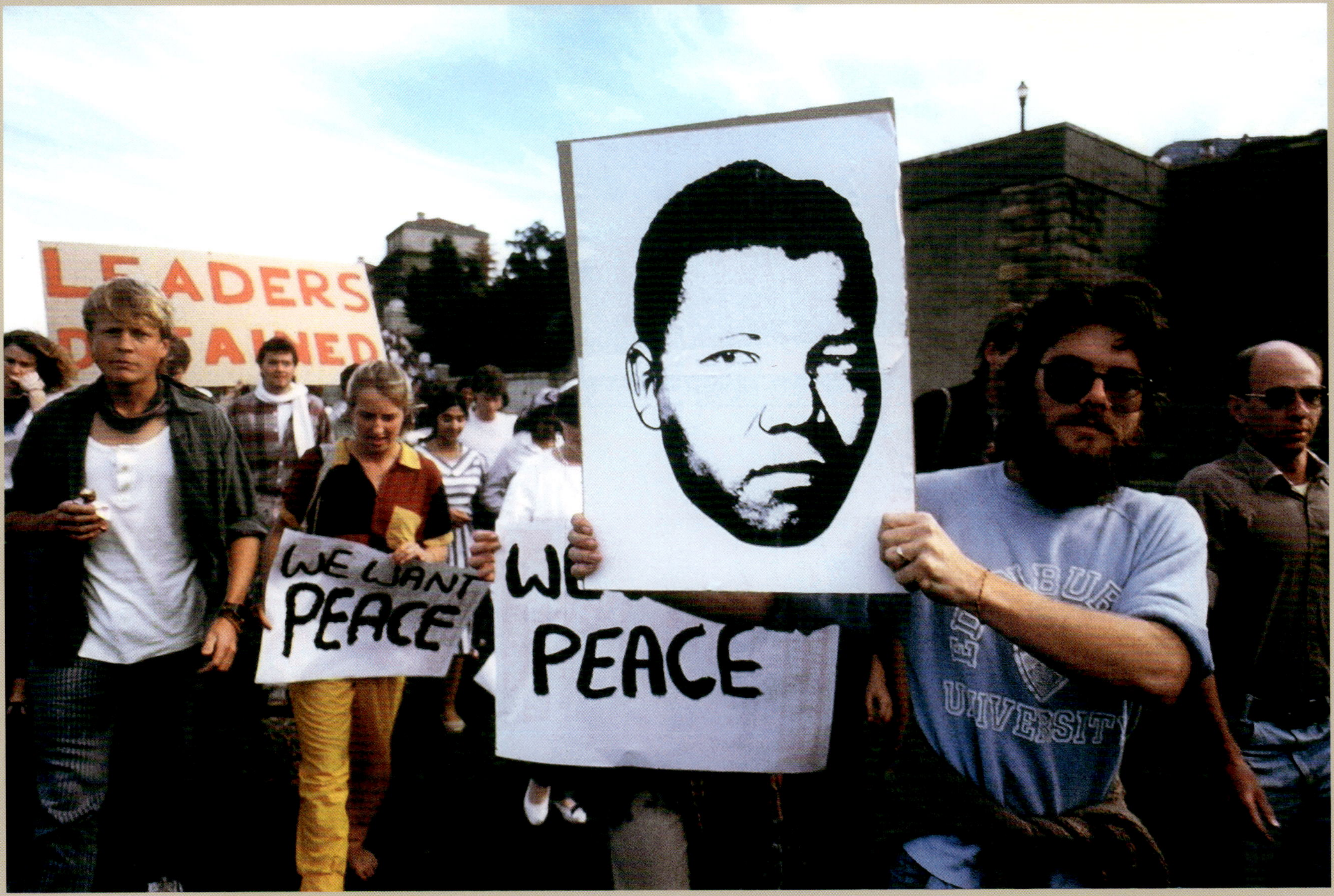
LEADERS
WE WANT PEACE
PEACE

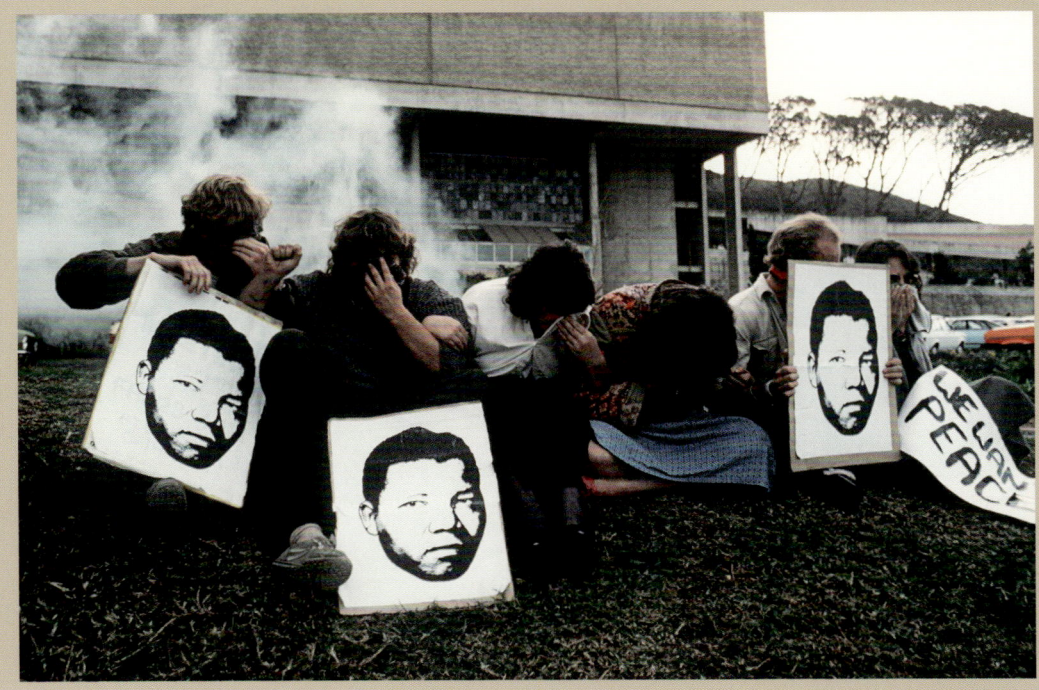

A protest march in Johannesburg against the banning of the United Democratic Front (UDF) and other organisations. The UDF emerged in the late 1980s until the release of political prisoners and the unbanning of the ANC and other political organisations.

The mass funeral for those massacred in Uitenhage on 21 March 1985.

LEFT: *Winnie, Zenani and Zindzi prior to their last visit to Pollsmoor prison before Nelson's transfer to Victor Verster.*

ABOVE: *This photograph was sent to Peter Magubane anonymously while he was working for* Time *magazine. The image shows Nelson Mandela, President P.W. Botha and senior government officials meeting at Victor Verster prison in Cape Town.*

THE FREEDOM YEARS

PREVIOUS PAGE: *Madiba shakes hands with a journalist on a morning walk in Washington DC.*

LEFT: *Nelson and Winnie in the gardens of Archbishop Desmond Tutu's residence in Bishopscourt, Cape Town, where Mandela spent his first night of freedom.*

FOLLOWING PAGE: *Cheering crowds wait to greet Nelson Mandela outside the City Hall in Cape Town on his first day of freedom, 11 February 1990.*

ABOVE LEFT: *Madiba's first phone call received after his release at his home in Orlando West, Soweto.*

BELOW LEFT: *Mandela, surrounded by his friends and family, toasts freedom shortly after his release.*

ABOVE: *Nelson and Winnie's first breakfast together at home after his release.*

LEFT: *The acclaimed author Ellen Kuzwayo praying at the Mandela home in Orlando West shortly after his release.*

ABOVE: *Nelson Mandela is embraced by Ina Perlman, the Managing Director of Operation Hunger, at his home in Orlando West.*

ABOVE: *Watched by his grandchildren, Mandela conducts a one-on-one interview with an international journalist at his home in Orlando West.*

RIGHT: *Madiba with the press at his home, No. 8115 Orlando West, Soweto.*

ABOVE THE CLAMOR, SOME VOICES RANG CLEAR—AND THE WORLD, AT LAST, WAS LISTENING

CRY FREEDOM

'We have waited too long for our freedom. We can no longer wait '

So said Nelson Mandela, symbol of South Africa's antiapartheid movement, on the day he was freed after 27 years, six months and a week in prison. Gripping wife Winnie's hand, Mandela walked through the gate of Victor Verster Prison at 4:15 in the afternoon to be welcomed by outpourings of black and white joy around the world. That evening he told a crowd of fellow South Africans, "To go to prison because of your convictions and be prepared to suffer for what you believe in is something worthwhile." (Mandela shares his personal memories of that day on page 86.) Such leaders—mythic figures willing to endure torture, harassment and imprisonment rather than forgo their ideals—emerge in troubled times. With power, dignity and triumphant humanity, the dissenters on these pages urged us forward. When each, like Mandela, lived to see a day of vindication, it was an achievement for us all.

RELEASED
February 11, 1990

ABOVE LEFT: *Madiba receives visitors at his home in Orlando West.*

BELOW LEFT: *Coco Cachalia, daughter of Amina and Yusuf Cachalia (leader of the South African Indian Congress), greets Nelson Mandela at his home during the first week of his release.*

BELOW RIGHT: *Mandela with students from the University of the Witwatersrand.*

ABOVE: *Nelson and Winnie at a function shortly after his release from prison.*

FOLLOWING PAGE: *Two of South Africa's Nobel Peace Prize Laureates, Nelson Mandela and Archbishop Desmond Tutu, join hands at Ipelegeng in White City, Soweto.*

LEFT: *An emotional Brenda Fassie, the South African pop diva, embraces Mandela.*

ABOVE: *Crowds gather at the FNB Stadium in Johannesburg to greet Mandela shortly after his release.*

Nelson and Winnie greet the crowds gathered at Ellis Park Stadium in Johannesburg to welcome him home.

Winnie and Nelson (holding Bambatha) in Qunu, Madiba's home village in the former Transkei. Mandela was visiting the grave of his mother who had passed away while he was in prison. He still has a house in Qunu where he enjoys time away with his family.

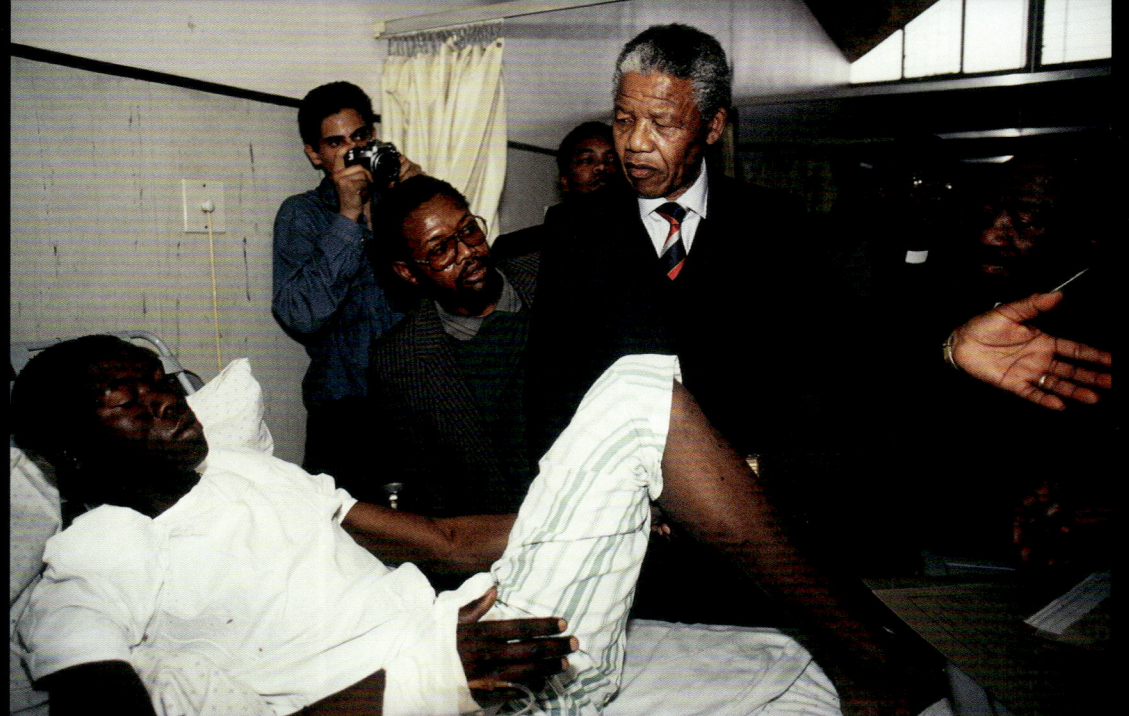

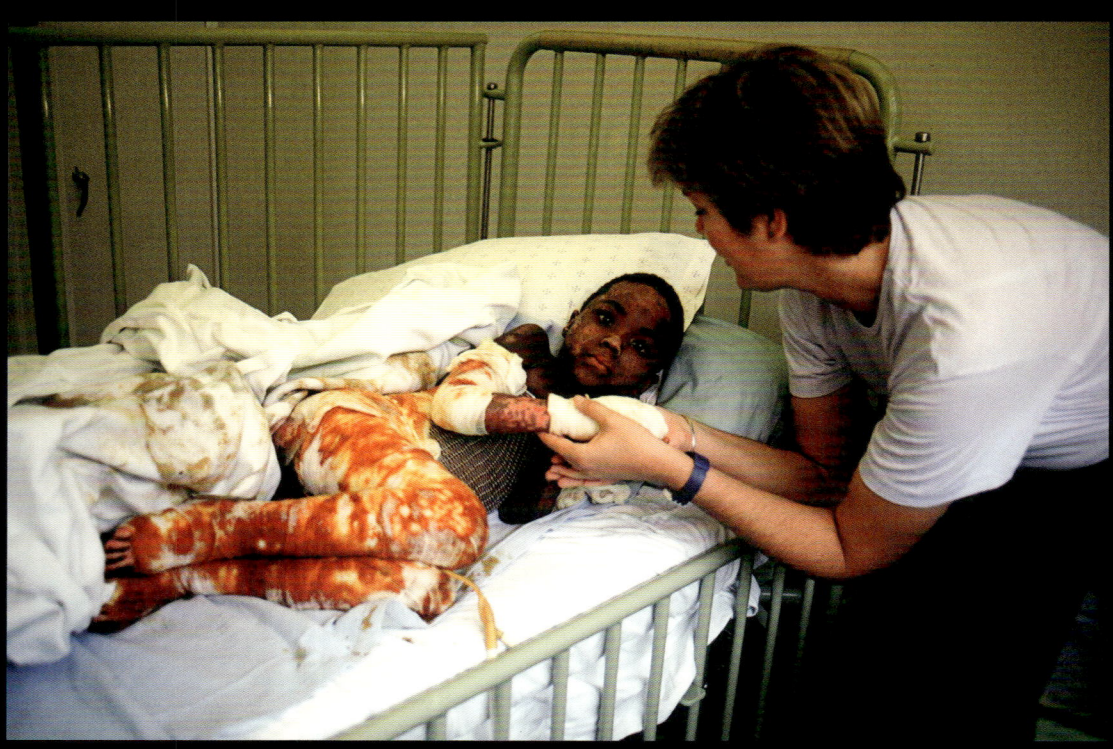

TOP: *Mandela visiting the injured at Sebokeng Hospital. Armed men went on a killing spree after a rally on 22 July 1990, murdering some thirty people.*

ABOVE: *A child injured in the black-on-black violence instigated by the police in Pietermaritzburg.*

ABOVE RIGHT: *The car of a suspected police informer is set alight in Duduza on the East Rand.*

BELOW RIGHT: *A policeman inspects a police car which was set alight outside Chris Hani's house. The Secretary-General of the South African Communist Party and former Chief of Staff of the ANC's armed wing Umkhonto we Sizwe (MK), Hani was shot at point-blank range in front of his home in Boksburg on 10 April 1993.*

ABOVE: *Nelson Mandela and President F.W. de Klerk walking to a press conference after the first meeting between the ANC and the National Party in Cape Town.*

RIGHT: *Mandela delivers a press statement to the world.*

TOP LEFT AND ABOVE: *Comrades reunited: Oliver Tambo and Nelson Mandela meet for the first time on South African soil since Tambo's return from thirty years of exile on 13 December 1990.*

BELOW LEFT: *A tender moment between Nelson and Winnie at a function with Oliver Tambo.*

LEFT: *Walter Sisulu with his wife Albertina shortly after his release from prison.*

ABOVE: *Walter Sisulu meets United States civil rights activist Jesse Jackson.*

ABOVE: *Tokyo Sexwale, Joe Slovo, Nelson Mandela and Cyril Ramaphosa in Soweto.*

RIGHT: *Thabo Mbeki, Nelson Mandela and President F.W. de Klerk at the opening of the last white parliament.*

ABOVE: *Nelson Mandela and Kenneth Kaunda meet in Zambia.*

LEFT: *Madiba and Queen Elizabeth II in Johannesburg.*

ABOVE RIGHT: *Madiba holds his first passport at his home in Orlando West.*

BELOW RIGHT: *Madiba meets Palestinian leader Yasser Arafat.*

ABOVE: *Waving flags greet Nelson and Winnie on their arrival at JFK Airport in New York.*

RIGHT: *Excited crowds gather to meet Mandela in New York City.*

ABOVE: *Tight security for Nelson and Winnie on their first state visit to New York in 1990.*

RIGHT: *Nelson Mandela addresses the crowds on his arrival at JFK Airport, New York. On his right are Harry Belafonte and his wife Julie.*

THE PORT AUTHORITY

TOP: *The Mayor of New York, David Dinkins, meets Nelson Mandela at JFK Airport.*

ABOVE: *Nelson Mandela meets Rosa Parks, the woman who was known as the 'mother of the civil rights movement', in Atlanta. Parks became famous for her refusal, on 1 December 1955, to obey bus driver James Blake's order that she give up her seat to make room for a white passenger.*

RIGHT: *Nelson and Winnie stroll in the gardens of the White House with President George Bush and First Lady Barbara Bush.*

ABOVE: *Nelson Mandela at the late Martin Luther King's home in Atlanta with (from left to right) Elder Bernice King, Winnie Mandela, Coretta Scott King, Martin King and Dexter King.*

LEFT: *Mandela with the Kennedy family (from right) Jack Kennedy Jnr, Jackie Onassis, Rose Kennedy and Senator Edward Kennedy.*

ABOVE RIGHT: *Mandela converses with United States civil rights activist Jesse Jackson in New York.*

BELOW RIGHT: *Nelson Mandela and musical icon Stevie Wonder in Washington DC.*

TOP: *Nelson Mandela's first address to the United Nations in New York.*

ABOVE LEFT: *Nelson Mandela with the former UN Secretary-General, Kofi Annan and his wife Nane in Johannesburg in 2007.*

ABOVE RIGHT: *Mandela meets the UN Secretary-General, Dr Pérez de Cuéllar, with the Mayor of New York, David Dinkins, and Winnie Mandela.*

TOP: *Muhammad Ali with Winnie and Nelson in New York.*

ABOVE: *Surrounded by heavyweights: Mike Tyson, Nelson Mandela, Don King, Sugar Ray Leonard,*
New York Mayor David Dinkins and Joe Frazier.

ABOVE LEFT: *Mandela and President F.W. de Klerk together at the Convention for a Democratic South Africa (CODESA), the formal negotiations held between parties at the World Trade Centre in Kempton Park, Johannesburg, to bring about the end of apartheid.*

FAR LEFT: *Mandela in the company of Walter Sisulu and Alfred Nzo.*

LEFT: *Zwelakhe Sisulu, Roelf Meyer, Nelson Mandela and Cyril Ramaphosa at the CODESA talks.*

ABOVE: *Mandela and Chief Mangosuthu Buthelezi, leader of the Inkatha Freedom Party.*

BELOW: *Nelson Mandela with Pik Botha, the Minister of Foreign Affairs in the National Party government.*

ABOVE: *Mandela talks to Chris Hani at the ANC conference in Durban.*

LEFT: *Mandela in close conversation with Helen Suzman, the veteran politician and anti-apartheid activist.*

ABOVE: *Walter Sisulu and Nelson Mandela at the ANC Conference in Durban 1990.*

RIGHT: *Nelson Mandela talks to Alfred Nzo at the ANC conference in Durban. Nzo was the longest-serving Secretary-General of the ANC.*

LEFT: *Support for Mandela and colleagues in Orlando East, Soweto.*

ABOVE: *Madiba visits his neighbours in Orlando West.*

FOLLOWING PAGE: *Madiba, in traditional furs, is welcomed by the women of Sharpeville.*

ABOVE: *Madiba and Dr Harry Seftel in Johannesburg. Seftel spent more than fifty years in the Department of Medicine at the University of the Witwatersrand – as a student, clinician, teacher, researcher and administrator.*

TOP RIGHT: *In 1994, Nelson Mandela revisited Robben Island, where he had spent nearly two decades in prison.*

BELOW RIGHT: *Former prisoners return for the first time to visit Robben Island.*

FAR RIGHT: *A warder shows visitors Mandela's jail cell on Robben Island.*

ABOVE: *Madiba greets well-wishers in Soweto.*

ABOVE RIGHT: *President Mandela with Miss USA, and Miss South Africa in the background, at the Miss World pageant, held at Sun City, outside Johannesburg, in November 2001.*

BELOW RIGHT: *Madiba with Laila Ali, professional boxer and daughter of the boxing champion Muhammad Ali, in Johannesburg in 2007.*

ABOVE: *Crowds of people travel to attend the funeral of Chris Hani held at the FNB Stadium.*
Hani was assassinated on 10 April 1993 outside his home in Dawn Park.

ABOVE RIGHT: *Chris Hani's wife, Limpho, and his three children attend the memorial service held on the first anniversary of his death.*

BELOW RIGHT: *President Mandela at the unveiling of Chris Hani's memorial on the first anniversary of his death.*

LEFT: *The ongoing violence in the 1990s meant that a dominant army presence was common to prevent uprisings around the election period.*

ABOVE: *President Nelson Mandela with fellow ANC member General Andrew Masondo. Both men are in MK uniform, as were many other former combatants gathered at Orlando Stadium.*

LEFT: *Beyers Naudé, the renowned Afrikaner cleric and anti-apartheid activist, outside Khotso House, the head office of the South African Council of Churches.*

FOLLOWING PAGE: *A peace rally in Cape Town in 1989.*

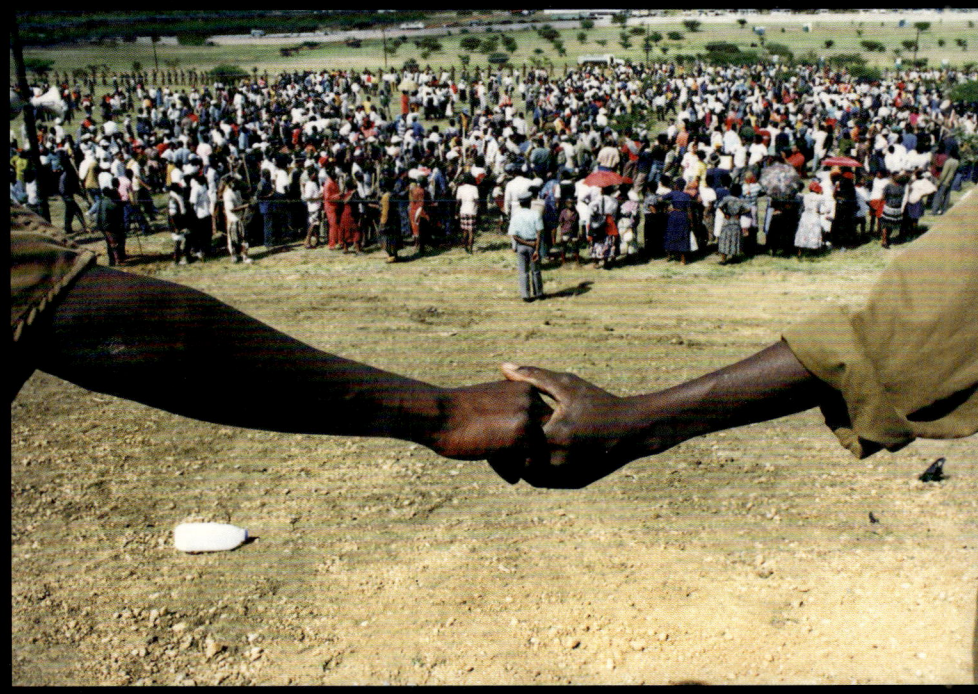

Inkatha Freedom Party supporters in Ulundi, KwaZulu-Natal.

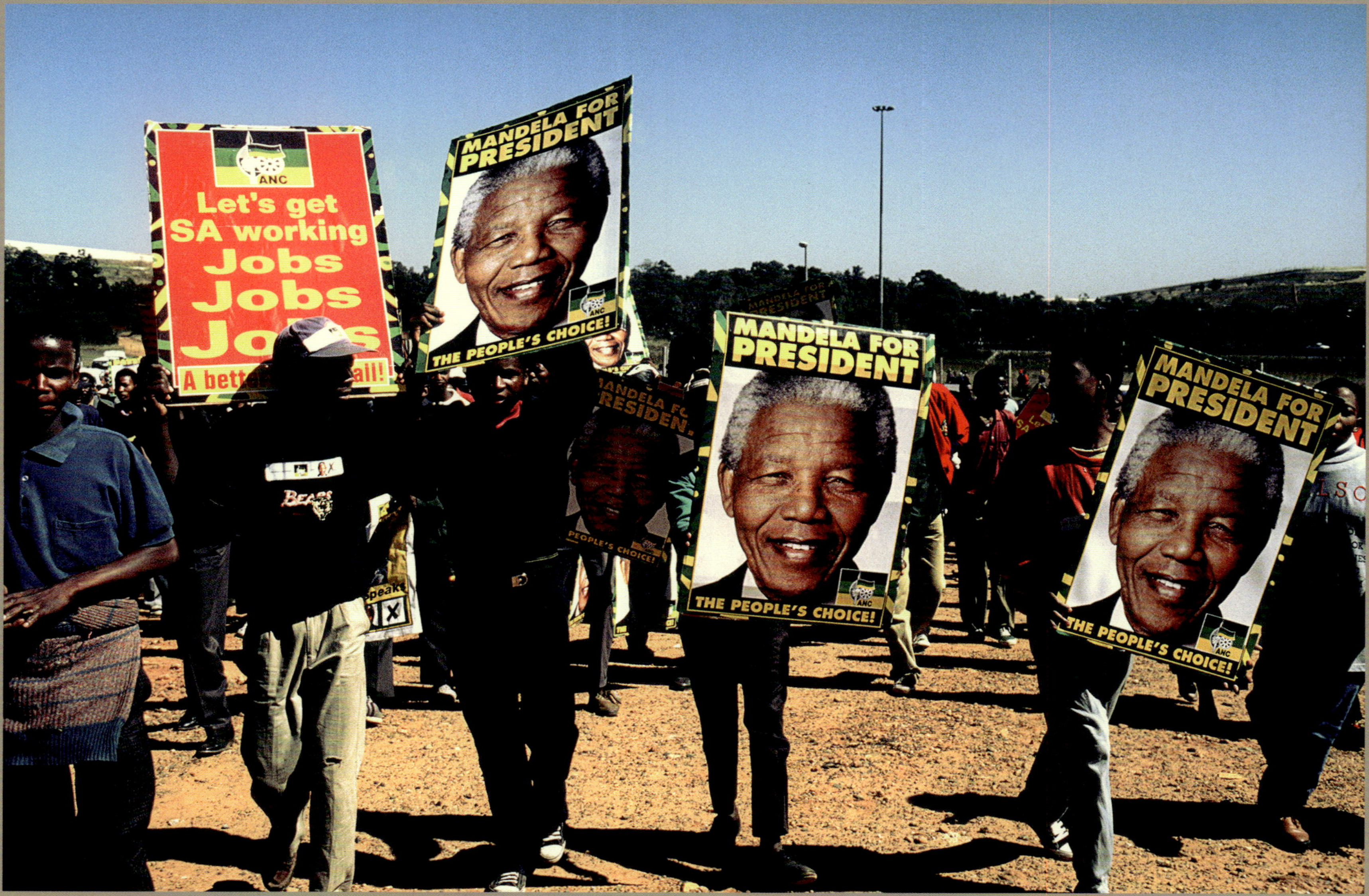
ANC
Let's get
SA working
Jobs
Jobs
MANDELA FOR
PRESIDENT
THE PEOPLE'S CHOICE!

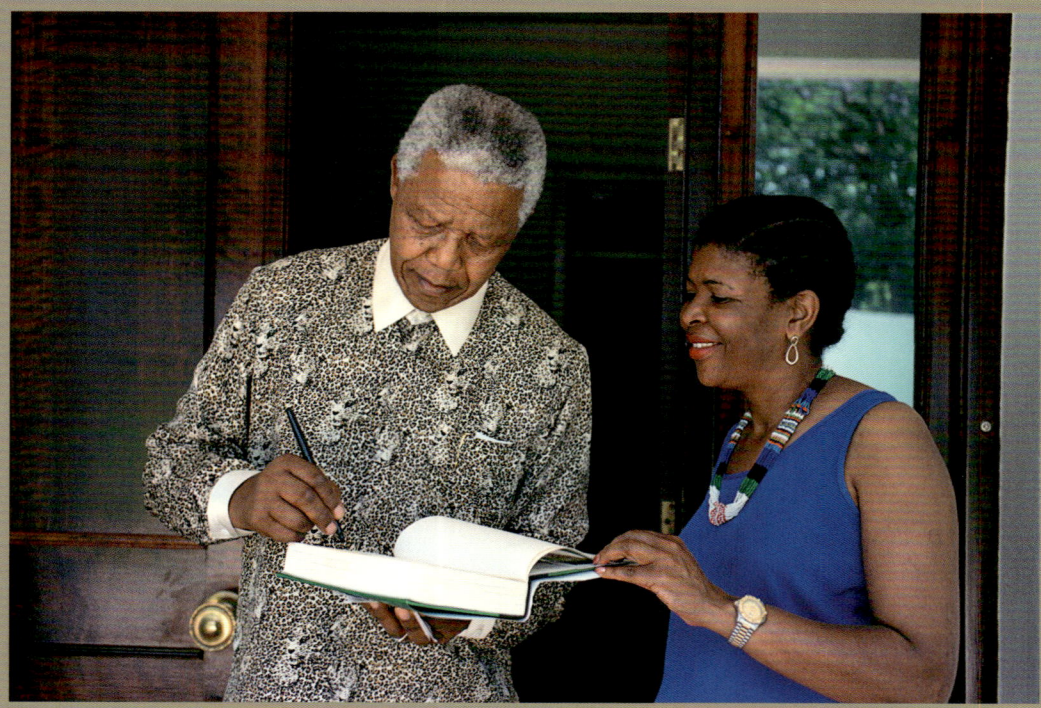

ABOVE LEFT: *Mandela for President: the people of Sharpeville make their choice known.*

BELOW LEFT: *Madiba signs Cindy Futhane's copy of his autobiography* Long Walk to Freedom. *Futhane was a member of the Independent Electoral Commission, the body appointed to oversee South Africa's first democratic election in 1994.*

ABOVE: *Supporters at an ANC rally in Bloemfontein shortly before the 1994 elections.*

Madiba laughs as his shoe comes off while kicking a soccer ball.

TOP LEFT: *Nelson Mandela arrives at the Zion Christian Church in City Moria, Polokwane.*

TOP RIGHT: *Madiba walks with Reverend Frans Mosese of the Zion Christian Church to attend the gathering in City Moria.*

ABOVE: *Reverend Frans Kekana, of the Alexandra Parish.*

RIGHT: *Members of the Zion Christian Church, the largest of the African independent churches, gather in City Moria.*

ABOVE: *Accompanying Nelson Mandela on one of his visits to KwaZulu-Natal in 1992 are, amongst others (from left to right), Josiah Jele, Joe Slovo, Dikgang Moseneke, Alfred Nzo and Gertrude Shope.*

RIGHT: *Madiba shakes hands with the Reverend Modise of the International Pentecostal Church and Bethuel Modise, the Reverend's eldest son.*

LEFT: *Mandela casts his vote in South Africa's first democratic elections on 27 April 1994 in Inanda, KwaZulu-Natal.*

ABOVE: *Jubilant South Africans celebrate the advent of democracy.*

ABOVE LEFT: *All South Africans join in the celebration of the election outcome at the Carlton Hotel in Johannesburg.*

BELOW LEFT: *Andrew Mlangeni, a former Robben Island prisoner, and Thabo Mbeki show their joy at the advent of democracy.*

ABOVE: *Youths in Soweto celebrate the ANC's first election victory.*

From left to right:
Mr and Mrs Schlebusch,
Jan van Vollenhoven,
Pik Botha and Mr and Mrs
Dawie de Villiers at the
presidential inauguration
in 1994.

The Mandela family gathered for a private function at Tuynhuys, the President's residence in Cape Town.

ABOVE: *Nelson stands with his daughters Zindzi, Zenani and Makaziwe and son Makgatho. Makaziwe and Makgatho are children from Mandela's first marriage to Evelyn Mase, whom he divorced in 1958.*

RIGHT: *Mandela proudly walks his daughter Zindzi down the aisle on her wedding day in October 1992.*

ABOVE LEFT: *Drum majorettes at the Union Buildings in Pretoria for the celebration of South Africa's first year of democracy.*

BELOW LEFT: *Mandela receives an Honorary Doctorate at the University of Witwatersrand in Johannesburg.*

ABOVE: *South African actress, Thembi Mtshali, dances at Mandela's 72nd birthday party.*

The much celebrated
'Madiba shuffle': Mandela
dances to Thandi Klaassens's
tune at his 72nd birthday
party at Kippies in
Johannesburg.

TOP: *Madiba celebrates his 72nd birthday, his first birthday since his release, with children at a crèche in Orlando West.*

ABOVE *A birthday cake fit for a President, adorned with doves of freedom.*

RIGHT: *President Mandela joins traditional dancers at his 75th birthday party.*

LEFT: *Madiba's 88th birthday celebrations at the Nelson Mandela Children's Fund offices in Johannesburg.*

ABOVE: *Eye-to-eye contact between Madiba and his grandson, Bambatha.*

ABOVE: *Madiba ponders an interview question.*

RIGHT: *Deep in thought: Madiba at the Pentecostal Church.*

LEFT: *Nelson Mandela celebrated his 80th birthday by marrying Graça Machel on 18 July 1998 in a private ceremony at his home in Houghton. Machel was formerly the wife of assassinated Mozambican President Samora Machel. Mandela had separated from his former wife Winnie in April 1992 and the two were divorced in March 1996.*

ABOVE: *Mandela with Makgatho, Zenani, his sister Leaby, Graça and Zindzi, on his wedding day.*

ABOVE: *Nelson and Graça at the cemetery after the funeral of Nelson's son, Makgatho, which was held in Qunu. Mandela's public declaration that Makgatho had died of HIV/AIDS had a positive effect on the fight against HIV/AIDS, a cause that is close to Madiba's heart.*

RIGHT: *Nelson and Graça's hands at Makgatho's funeral.*

*Madiba greets children
in Boipatong.*

Nelson Mandela with his great-granddaughter, Pumla, in September 1994.

ABOVE: *Mandela at Oliver Tambo's funeral at St Mary's Anglican Church in Johannesburg. At Mandela's request, Tambo was given a state funeral. MK troops marched in his honour and a 21-gun salute was performed at his graveside.*

LEFT: *Crowds gathered at Oliver Tambo's funeral.*

ABOVE RIGHT: *Madiba at the funeral of his long-standing friend and comrade, Walter Sisulu, at the Orlando Stadium on 5 May 2003.*

BELOW RIGHT: *Madiba and Makhenkesi Arnold Stofile at Walter Sisulu's funeral at Orlando Stadium.*

TOGETHER

FIGHTING FOR
CHANGE
A better life for all. Vote ANC

In a jubilant mood: the newly elected President Thabo Mbeki and Nelson Mandela at the Orlando Stadium in Soweto.

RIGHT: *Nelson with Winnie and Graça at Christmas lunch in 2004.*

FOLLOWING PAGE: *Graça, Madiba, Zindzi and Winnie at Zindzi's birthday party in 2007.*

Nelson Mandela being awarded the Freedom of the City of Tshwane, at the Nelson Mandela Foundation in Johannesburg, 13 May 2008. On the left is Geraldine Fraser-Moleketi and on the right is Dr Gwen Ramokgopa.

ODE TO MY FATHER

Zindzi Mandela

Tata

I can imagine
> What you would be
> If I was not
> What you would say
> If I kept quiet

I can imagine
> Where you would go
> If I remained
> Where you would end
> If I started

I can imagine
> What you would admire
> If I was disgusted
> What you would love
> If I only hated

I can imagine
> What you would enjoy
> If I felt depressed
> What you would do
> If I did not

This poem was written by Nelson Mandela's daughter in 1972, when she was twelve years old.